Evans

Practical

Handbooks

General Editor: Charles H. Hayward

House Decoration

HOUSE
DECORATION

A. VERNON LOVEGROVE, F.R.S.A.

10 years Teacher of Painting and Decorating,
Reading Technical College
Lecturer in House Repairs to L.E.A. Evening classes

Evans Brothers Limited
Montague House, Russell Square, London W.C.1

First published 1962

© Evans Brothers Limited 1962

Printed in Great Britain by Cox and Wyman Ltd., London, Reading and Fakenham.
[7/5448]

Contents

Introduction

Never before has there been such a general interest in attractive homes and such a conscious desire to achieve good decoration by simple means. Inspired by the colourful designs in the glossy magazines and fascinated by the alluring settings for plays seen on television and on colour films, the urge for good decoration has percolated through to the home.

It is with the increasing number of house-owners that the great movement towards practical beauty is being quietly carried on. Clean bright colours have replaced the eternal dark browns and greens, while the coming of 'do it for yourself' has opened new vistas of contemporary decoration.

This handbook explains the techniques of practical house decoration—the means to an end—which will enable the home decorator to interpret ideas compatible with the ever increasing demand for more elegant surroundings.

The author of this handbook is both an artist and an experienced craftsman. He is a member of the Reading Guild of Artists, and has conducted successfully his own business as a builder and decorator since 1917. The contents are based on his own practical experiences which have been tempered and enriched by the part-time teaching of painting and decorating apprentices. It has a strong practical bias with emphasis on method and the correct procedure of doing a worthwhile job properly. It is designed to assist the apprentice, the house painter and the owner, through technical ability and knowledge, to satisfaction and pleasure in designing and executing the humblest and the most elaborate decorative schemes.

N. W. Kay, A.I.Struct.E., M.R.San.I., A.I.W.Sc., F.R.S.A.

Head of Department of Building,
Reading Technical College.

1 Reasons for Painting Materials and Equipment

ALTHOUGH PERHAPS all trades are equally important in building construction, the final appearance and durability of any structure depends almost entirely upon the care and skill of the decorator. Since a large proportion of buildings consists of metal and timber, liable to corrosion and decay, the principal reason for painting must be that of *Preservation*. This can only be achieved by suitable preparation, and the application of priming and protective finishing coats.

Next in order of precedence should come *Hygiene*. Most building materials are absorbent to a greater or lesser degree and a correctly applied paint system provides smooth, impervious surfaces, readily resistant to dirt and easily cleaned when necessary. The importance of this in kitchens and bathrooms, hospitals ot shops and offices is obvious. The provision of legislation in the interest of clean food and sanitary living and working conditions are evidence of the regard of Parliament for the requirements of health and well-being.

Thirdly, *Decoration*. Suitable colour schemes, harmonious design and imaginative decor should all play their part in achieving attractive environments for living, working, and playing. From earliest times, man has decorated his dwelling, from the cave paintings of France, Spain, and Africa, the ancient Egyptian temples and tombs, and so on right through the ages. Even the ancient Greek temples and our early stone churches were coloured, and the urge for mankind to embellish both themselves and their surroundings appears almost instinctive.

These functions overlap in practice, the combination of protection and attractive decoration being readily achieved. The successful application of paint for any purpose depends on a thorough knowledge of materials, preparation and application, and equipment.

MATERIALS

Older text books deal at length with the formulation of paints, but nowadays manufacturers supply such excellent and varied paints, ready mixed for all purposes, that, except for the research student, such detailed knowledge is

9

largely superfluous. However, some knowledge of the composition of the material to be used is essential to ensure the correct selection of the paint and the technique involved in application for specific purposes.

How Paint Dries

Ordinary oil paints dry by the absorption of oxygen from the atmosphere by the drying oil, such as linseed, the only evaporation being from the thinners. Anything which stops the combination of the oil with oxygen prevents drying.

The medium or vehicle is a drying oil or oils in which are incorporated various natural and/or synthetic resins and gums. The oil on exposure to the air forms a transparent, elastic, and durable film which binds the particles of pigment together.

Pigments

These pigments, in the case of white, are carbonates, oxides and sulphides of lead, zinc, antimony, titanium, etc., which readily mix and in some cases chemically combine with the drying oil and materially assist its durability. Pigments possess varying properties and degrees of whiteness. White lead is pre-eminent for its lasting properties and the ease with which it may be re-coated, titanium oxide for its extreme whiteness and opacity. Often a combination is used to ensure best results, the rather soft and elastic white lead being hardened by the addition of zinc oxide and opacity augmented with titanium.

Coloured pigments are again usually metallic compounds. Yellow is often a compound of lead, chromium, and oxygen, or a clay containing a hydrate of iron. Prussian blue contains iron, carbon, nitrogen, and oxygen, and has the terrifying chemical name of ferric-ferro cyanide. Many permanent dye stuffs are used, such as the beautiful and permanent monastral blue and hansa yellow. Red lead is an oxide of lead, notable for the way in which it assists the oxidation of the oil, forming a hard yet elastic rust inhibiting primer for iron and steel.

Thinners

Thinners are volatile spirits, such as turpentine or white spirit. Genuine turpentine is prepared by distilling the resinous sap of coniferous trees, and white spirit or 'turps sub.', a refined petroleum of high flash point prepared by the fractional distillation of crude petroleum. These are used to adjust the paint to a proper working consistency, acting as a solvent for the medium only and evaporating completely. For most purposes today there is no apparent advantage in using the more expensive genuine turpentine, indeed often the contrary. The varying proportions of pigment, vehicle, and thinners decide the amount of gloss, preponderance of vehicle producing high gloss, and a greater percentage of pigment or thinners gives flat paints. Flat and semi-gloss paints are rich in pigment, sharp undercoats rich in thinners.

Driers and Extenders

Driers, again chemical compounds of metals and oxygen, are added to expedite drying time. They function by a complicated process of transference of oxygen to the medium, but excess can be dangerous, literally burning the paint away over a period.

Extenders are added for various purposes. They are inert materials of no or little colour and may be used to increase abrasive resistance, e.g. silica; or

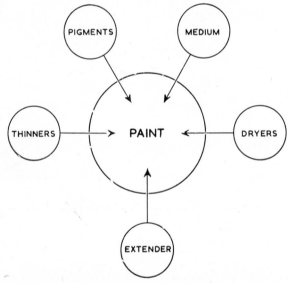

Fig. 1. PAINT AND ITS CONSTITUENTS.

adhesiveness, e.g. mica; moisture resistance, e.g. silicones. Dyes and some coloured pigments lack body, and this may be supplied by the addition of barytes giving 'body' to the paint without altering the hue or shade, such as would result from the addition of an opaque pigment. Unfortunately, extenders are sometimes added merely to increase the bulk and cheapen the paint, so beware of so-called bargain prices.

Modern paint chemistry is exceedingly complex, but with strict compliance with printed instructions by reputable manufacturers, nothing should

11

go wrong. In case of doubt, most makers will prepare a specification on receipt of detailed requirements and on larger jobs of a difficult nature will often send a technical expert to advise. On large contracts it is not unusual for these experts to supervise the contract on behalf of the building owner, thus ensuring that their product gets the best chance of success.

Distemper

Washable distemper is nowadays compounded from pigments, the white base usually lithopone (a zinc sulphate-barium sulphide) and titanium and bound with a drying oil emulsion. The oil such as linseed is intimately mixed with water in the presence of size or an alkali, violently agitated together until the oil and water become compatible, forming a stable emulsion which may be thinned by the addition of water as required. The mixture dries by evaporation of the water and oxidation of the oil. As this latter process takes some time, ample intervals must be allowed between coats.

Soft or ceiling distempers are compounded from whiting (refined chalk) and glue size with added preservative. These are easily applied opaque washes mixed with water and are equally easily removed. The modern plastic emulsions are misnamed. Strictly speaking they are bound with dispersions of finely divided synthetic resins such as poly-vinyl acetate in water. On drying these coalesce and bind the pigment to the surface. Adhesion is not so good as with oil-bound water paints, but these so-called emulsions have two distinct advantages; rapid drying with the possibility of re-coating within a few hours, and resistance to attack from alkalinity present in new plasters.

Special Paints

Cement paints are usually made from white and tinted Portland cements with various stabilizing and adhesive additives. Lime wash is made by slaking quick lime and should be used while still hot. Tallow and salt are sometimes added to improve adhesion. Stone paints usually contain powdered stone incorporated in special media. The makers' recommended thinners should always be used. Many special paints, such as chlorinated rubber are available for specific purposes. Bitumen paints, obtainable in colours, though rather subdued, as well as the standard black are useful coatings for ironwork to sheds, etc., and as a paint for plinths.

TOOLS

Brushes

To attempt to use the best of paints with poor tools would be foolish, as results depend entirely on the quality of materials, preparation, and application. This means that the best tools and good brushes, though expensive, are an economy in the long run. Modern paint brushes are usually flat in shape. They should consist of hog bristle, grey, white or black, of suitable length, securely mounted with *vulcanized* rubber or synthetic resin glue in a rustless metal ferrule attached to a polished wood handle, shapely and well balanced.

When purchasing a brush, bunch the bristles together in the hand. This will reveal the fullness or sparsity (see Fig. 2). Spring the bristles by turning over against the hand and releasing to test spring. Pure bristle is 'flagged', (D, Fig. 2), and good eyesight shows the split ends which hold the droplets of paint and prevent drips and splashes. This can be imitated in cheap hair and fibre, but wears away in use. Continued use of good bristle results in continued flagging as the brush wears down.

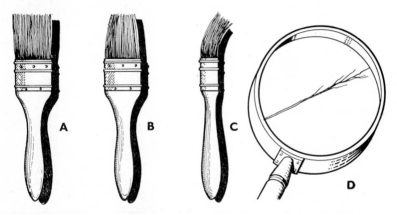

Fig. 2. FEATURES OF PAINT BRUSHES. A. Normal brush. B. Bristles bunched. C. Bristles sprung. D. Enlarged bristle showing flagged end.

Brush Sizes

Paint brushes are described by width and are obtainable in sizes of $\frac{1}{2}$ in., $\frac{3}{4}$ in., 1 in., $1\frac{1}{2}$ in., 2 in., $2\frac{1}{2}$ in., 3 in., and 4 in. For small work $\frac{3}{4}$ in. to 2 in. are suitable; others to requirements. Too small a brush involves too many strokes and uneven application; too large results in clumsiness and, with very stiff paints, unnecessarily hard work. Best work is always achieved with the optimum sized and quality brush. For small cutting-in a worn brush should be used, confining a new brush to broader work, thus breaking it in to a chisel edge ready to replace the other when worn out. Figs. 3 and 4 show a range of brushes.

The best brush for cutting in sash bars and the like is the round sash tool. Sizes are by number, 2, 3, 4, 6, 8, and 10. They need bridling with string to about half the length of the bristle, shortening the effective length to ensure adequate control. The tool should be used in such a way that a chisel edge or bevel is formed. This is maintained by lessening the tied-up portion, and thus exposing the same effective length of bristle until the bridle is no longer required. When it reaches this stage, it is time to commence breaking in a new brush, using the old for fine work until useless. Cutting the point off then provides a quite useful stencil brush and so nothing is wasted.

Distemper brushes are of two kinds, flat and round. The latter are usually two-knot, rarely three- or four-knot. For modern distempers and emulsion paints flat brushes are economical, spreading an even wash. For old fashioned and soft distempers, uneven and absorbent surfaces, the two-knot brush has definite advantages. Nylon fibre is now being used with some success, especially in flat distemper brushes. It wears exceedingly well but lacks the elasticity and some of the cleanliness of the best bristle. The nylon fibre is artificially flagged, but after breaking in, the eventual absence of flags does not seem to result in excessive spattering.

Flat brushes are listed by width, 4 in., 5 in., 6 in., and 7 in., with corresponding weights in ounces of the bristles. The length out is also specified with a good brush. Two-knot brushes are listed by weight and length of bristle, i.e. 8 oz., 10 oz., etc., length out 5 in. to 6 in. They may be either mounted with copper wire or ferrules.

Round and oval paint brushes are still obtainable, and require bridling like sash tools. They possess excellent qualities for covering large areas of metal, especially with straight oil paints, but are expensive, needing all the care that an experienced craftsman can bestow. Duster brushes are like small distemper brushes. Quality varies according to price, and a cheap hair or nylon brush proves expensive by reason of its ineffectiveness in flicking out adhesive dust from corners. If set in pitch instead of vulcanized rubber, they must never come into contact with turps.

Small long-handled brushes are known as fitches. They should be of hog hair, mounted in tin ferrules and the right length and section for their purpose. Fitches for striking lines are bevelled, and flat or round fitches are used for various decorative and small detail. Sign writers' brushes and pencils, flat and round, are made from pure red sable hair mounted in quill or ferrule. Those in quill are designated in sizes progressively as lark, crow, small duck, duck, large duck, small goose, goose, ex goose, small swan, and swan. Pencils in ferrule have numbers from 0 to 12.

Brushes for limewhiting and the application of caustic materials are made from fibre, and often colloquially called grass brushes. Alkali rapidly destroys bristle, and acids attack synthetic fibres in varying degrees. Special brushes used for paperhanging, graining and marbling, stencilling, and gilding, etc. will be more appropriately described in the relevant sections of this book. Stippling brushes should be of hog hair or of rubber for coarser work,

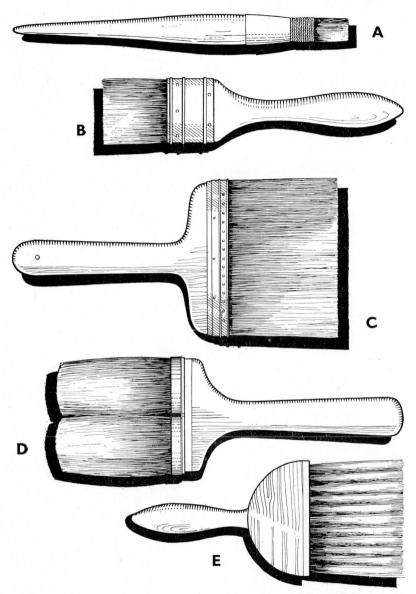

Fig. 3. TYPICAL PAINT AND DISTEMPER BRUSHES. A. Round sash tool with bristles shortened by hip binding with string. B. Flat paint brush, also used for varnishing. C. Flat distemper or wall brush. D. Two-knot distemper brush. E. Jamb duster brush.

15

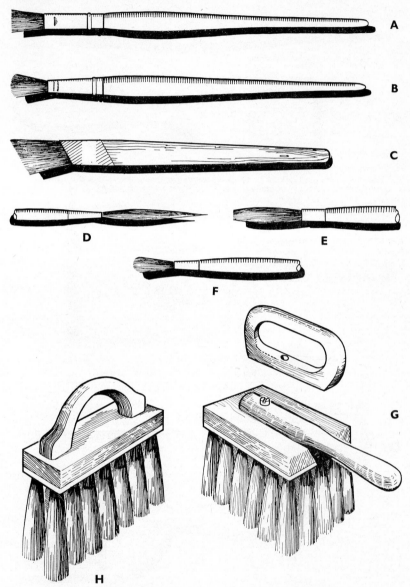

Fig. 4. VARIOUS BRUSHES USED BY THE DECORATOR. A and B. Flat and round fitches. C. Bristle lining tool. D. Liner. E. Writer. F. Pencil. G. and H. Stippling brushes.

preferably with reversible handles. These are used for obtaining fine to coarse even textures by beating the paint.

Steel Tools

A variety of steel tools is required as shown in Fig. 5. They should be of good quality and preferably with the steel tang anchored right through the handle,

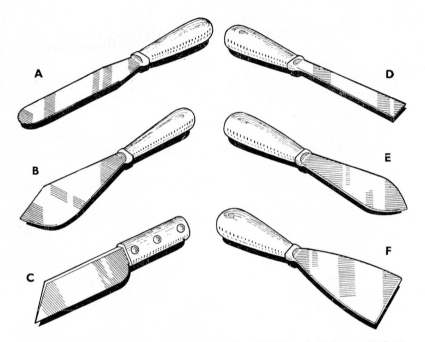

Fig. 5. VARIOUS KNIVES USED IN DECORATING.   A. Palette.   B. Putty.
C. Hacking.   D. Chisel.   E. Stopping.   F. Filling.

which should be of ebonite or suitable hardwood. Tools for special crafts will be described in appropriate context, but every painter's kit should include putty and stopping knives, stripping, chisel, filling, palette and hacking knives, and shave hooks.

Besides these he should have pincers, pliers, screwdrivers, bradawl, punch, hammer, wood chisel, and trowel. These and others of the like are all considered requisites of the operative, the employer being responsible for general equipment and expendables such as brushes, sponges, etc. A stout

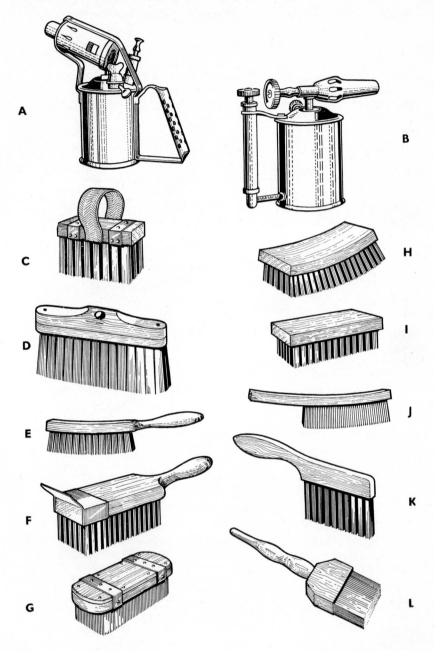

case, equipped with suitable compartments adequately stocked with clean tools is one of the hall-marks of the good craftsman, in contrast to the 'putty knife and stripper only man'.

Materials and Apparatus for Cleaning Down

Preparation work requires various grades of wet or dry glasspaper, pumice and artificial pumice blocks, sponges, natural and cellulose, chamois leathers, rubbing blocks for holding glasspaper, galvanized pails and kettles, etc. Paint kettles are best galvanized and are of varying diameters from 4 in. upwards. A stout wire S hook is useful for suspending a kettle from a ladder rung, and a heavy screw eye for screwing into soffits to provide anchorage for tying a ladder securely.

Blow lamps for burning off are obtainable for use with paraffin or petrol. On the whole paraffin lamps tend to give a longer trouble-free life, though both are a pest at times. Butane lamps are trouble free, igniting instantly, but refills are expensive. Various gas appliances are available, but present the difficulty of long trailing tubes from generator or cylinder to burner. Wire brushes for cleaning off rust and rough incrustations are also needed.

A form of stout hacking knife is useful for chipping off rust, and shave hooks with triangular, heart, and moulded shaped heads are indispensable for burning off. Most painters acquire a variety of improvised gadgets, all of which prove their worth.

Paint strainers are supplied with detachable copper meshed gauzes of varying degrees of fineness.

General Equipment

This consists of ladders, steps, trestles, planks, cripples and ladder brackets, hawks, putty boards, palettes, brooms, dust sheets, and so on. All should be the best of their respective kinds and of suitable size. The modern extension ladder, varying in height from 12 to 60 feet for two section and up to 90 feet for three section, is much more adaptable than the old fashioned pole ladder of which perhaps four or more would be required to do the work of one extension.

A useful adjunct is a ladder bracket which is affixed to the top rungs. It keeps the ladder about eighteen inches away from the wall, thus enabling work to be carried out easily and safely to projecting eaves and the like

Fig. 6. (*opposite*). EQUIPMENT REQUIRED IN DECORATING. A. Paraffin blow lamp. B. Petrol blow lamp. C–L. Various wire brushes. C has wrist strap, D is for broom attachment, and F has useful scraper attachment.

(see Fig. 7). Brackets for supporting planks, known as cripples (Fig. 8), may also be secured to rungs at convenient heights, making sure that both supporting ladders are fully secured top and bottom.

Safety regulations should be strictly observed. These state that all ladders over 8 feet high must be secured at the top and planking of this height must be at least two boards (18 in.) wide. Special regulations apply to all scaffolds, ensuring stability and safety guard rails, toe boards, etc. For large jobs it is much more economical to use steel scaffolding which can be hired from specialist firms who estimate for and erect the necessary tubes and boards.

Washing facilities should be provided on every job, as many paints are exceedingly poisonous. Clean hands are essential before eating a meal and soiled protective clothing removed when knocking off.

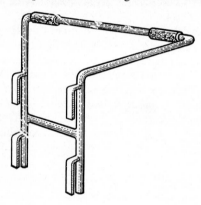

Fig. 7. EASY-REACH LADDER STAY.

Paint Shop

The elaborate paint shops of yesterday are now seldom required. However, a well-lit shop with a sufficiently large bench, preferably with a non-absorbent top, is necessary; also adequate shelving, cupboards and drawers, and sink with hot and cold. Storage arrangements for oil and turps, bins for cleaning rags, plasters, flour, etc., as well as refuse should be available in strategic positions. An old tank filled with caustic soda solution is useful for pickling dirty paint kettles which may well remain in soak directly after return from a job, then scrubbed clean and replaced with more from the next job. If work is carried out in the shop itself, adequate racks and easels should occupy well-lit and convenient positions.

Maintenance

All tools and equipment should be maintained in a scrupulously clean and sound condition. Brushes must be cleaned after use. Oil paint brushes should

Fig. 8. Close-up view of boards resting on cripples. See note on safety regulations given on page 34.

be suspended in water overnight. If not required for some time they should be washed out in detergent or one of the modern cleansers and stored, wrapped in paper to prevent moth attack. Soiled dust sheets should be laundered as soon as opportune and scaffold regularly overhauled. Items beyond satisfactory repair should be scrapped. To arrive on a job with clean utensils and scaffold creates an immediate good impression, while on the other hand no householder welcomes the evidence of other peoples dirt being introduced into their homes. Cleanliness is next to Godliness, a precept which should be observed in carrying out what is sometimes unavoidably a dirty job.

2 Preparation

CORRECT PREPARATION is perhaps the most important stage in producing a good and durable finish. No amount of subsequent rubbing down, scraping, and touching up will remedy early omissions and, indeed, may sometimes make matters worse. Coat after coat of distemper or paint add stresses and strains which eventually result in a breakdown. Take for an example an ordinary ceiling. Each successive coat may need 7 lb. of distemper. To apply two coats on four successive occasions means that there is half a hundred-weight suspended from the plaster. If original adhesion is poor, due to faulty preparation, flaking is inevitable.

Similar stresses and strains arise from temperature and moisture variations, and gravity is by no means the only force involved. Layers of dirt, grease, or polish between coats prevent adhesion, as does also the attempt to superimpose new paint over a glossy non-absorbent surface. With new work it is essential that perfect adhesion is obtained by proper preparation and priming with the correct type of primer for the particular surface. With old work, all doubtful films should be removed and the remainder thoroughly rubbed down and cleansed. All surfaces must be perfectly dry and neutral before priming.

Exterior Work

This provides the greatest test, exposure being as severe as our notorious weather can make it. With new work all timber should be primed before fixing, preferably before assembly. Softwoods should be lightly glasspapered, dusted off, and two coats of patent knotting thinly applied to all knots. Rub

Fig. 1. WASHING DOWN WALL WHICH, APART FROM DIRT, IS IN GOOD CONDITION.

down lightly between coats, touching up the second coat with sharp white. Knotting is a solution of shellac in commercial alcohol or methylated spirit, and in some measure prevents the exudation of resin which, being soluble in paint media and thinners, would otherwise take place.

Large or loose knots should be cut out and replaced by sound timber glued in. When all is dry the work should be brush primed with a good red and white lead primer. Cheap, so-called pink primers may contain little or

23

no lead and are of no value. Very resinous woods are best treated with an aluminium primer which has special sealing and adhesive qualities. Hardwoods should be treated with a rather thin long oil primer.

Cleaning Down

Previously painted woodwork in sound condition should be washed and rubbed down to a smooth surface. Greasy work should be washed with hot water containing sugar soap or other paint cleaner made up to conform with the printed directions on the packet. While wet it should be rubbed down with wet or dry glasspaper, pumice stone (this can easily be sawn to give a flat surface), artificial pumice blocks, or steel wool. The small surfaces are best dealt with by using waterproof paper or steel wool, reserving the block or pumice for the large flats. If using steel wool, make sure that all residue is removed, as small fragments may rust and cause stains through the new paint.

Always commence at the bottom, working up, to avoid runs of concentrated cleaner which might soften the paint in streaks. Small, isolated blisters may be removed by thorough scraping, but if these are at all numerous, approaching breakdown is indicated, and complete stripping or burning off must be undertaken. After rubbing down, rinse with plenty of clean cold water, sponge and leather off dry, making sure that no residue remains in the quirks of mouldings. With very greasy work, the addition of about 5 per cent methylated spirits to the rinsing water is sometimes advantageous.

The function of the rubbing down is twofold; to ensure a relatively smooth and even surface, and also to microscopically roughen it to provide a key for succeeding coats. It is especially important to break down the hard glossy film of old paints.

Burning Off

Complete removal necessitates burning off or the use of a paint remover. Burning off in skilled hands is much quicker and cheaper, and if accomplished without charring or other damage, is most efficient. To ignite a paraffin lamp, fill about three-quarters full, and tightly replace the filler cap, open the air release valve, fill the priming dish with methylated spirit, and apply a lighted match. Failing methylated spirit, use paraffin with a small piece of rag to act as a wick, as the oil will not burn on its own. The use of meth. keeps the lamp much cleaner.

The lighted primer heats the coil and burner, converting the liquid paraffin to gas. Just before the priming fluid has burnt out, close the air release valve and give a couple of pumps. A violet-blue flame should commence, and this can be increased by further pumping, or decreased by momentarily

Fig. 2. USING SHAVE HOOK TO REMOVE OLD PAINT FROM MOULDING
AFTER HEATING WITH BLOW LAMP.

opening the air release valve. If a yellow flame results or liquid oil shoots out (never align the lamp on inflammable material) further priming is necessary.

Never attempt to light a lamp in a draught. If no flame appears, do not persist with pumping. This may be dangerous as it is probably due to a choked nipple. This may be cleared with a pricker specially made for the purpose. In obstinate cases it may be necessary to remove the nipple with a nipple key, a long rod slotted at the end to fit over the square shoulder of the nipple. When replacing be careful that the thread is not crossed. It pays to give a couple of pumps when the nipple is out, to flush out the coil.

Before commencing to burn off, all movable fittings, such as letter plates, etc., should be detached and carefully put aside, nuts being replaced temporarily. Curtains should also be removed from the inside, and, of course, carpets and rugs. If working over a wood or easily damaged fixed floor covering, a thin sheet of metal or asbestos should be inserted underneath, and an old pail kept handy to receive the scrapings. The added precaution of a pail of water has sometimes prevented disaster. Mouldings should be tackled first by heating until blistered, playing the lamp backwards and forwards or up and down for about a foot at a time, then scraping with a suitably shaped shave hook or chisel knife. As heat rises, commence at the bottom and work upwards, thus avoiding charring surfaces already stripped. Fig. 2 shows the process.

The larger flat surfaces (again commencing at the bottom) should be removed with the stripping knife. Gently follow the flame of the lamp which should always be directed on the paint film and never on the bare wood as in Fig. 3. A little practice will show the speed with which to move the flame and following knife according to the thickness and resistance of the paint. With really obstinate films it may be necessary to use a shave hook, scraping instead of pushing the stripping knife. The writer has had occasion to remove the accumulation of three centuries, resulting in over 300 separate coatings, and careful scraping followed by successive heatings and scrapings, was the only possible technique.

Complete removal without charring the wood is usually impossible, though no paint as such should be allowed to remain. Once it has all been loosened, however, it may be removed by the next process, that of dry scraping with shave hook or patent scraper. This scraping should be methodically carried out over the whole work, with particular attention paid to particles remaining in quirks, mitres, and adjoining locks, etc. Steel wool or the gentle use of a wire brush helps with mouldings. This scraping should leave the work reasonably smooth, and avoids clogging the glasspaper.

Glasspapering

To comply with regulations governing the use of white lead, the glasspaper should be moistened with white spirit thus obviating flying dust. Unfortunately this provision is seldom observed as dry rubbing down is much more efficient. Use coarse paper first, following with fine, and work methodically,

Fig. 3. FLAT SURFACE BEING STRIPPED USING BLOW LAMP AND STRIPPING KNIFE.

testing the smoothness with the ball of the thumb. Never burn off more than can be rubbed down and primed before the advent of rain, and never leave work unprimed overnight. Burning off renders the wood perfectly dry and ready to absorb the priming. The effects of even a slight shower may take days to eliminate. Imprisoned moisture is bound to form blisters.

The procedure with a petrol lamp is similar, but the flame is regulated by turning a knob which controls a needle valve, there being no air release valve. Extreme care is necessary with such an explosive and inflammable fuel. Some petrol lamps are equipped with a pump, this should be used with discretion and if there is any doubt the nipple should be cleaned. Pumpless lamps only maintain pressure from the expansion due to heat and may need occasional re-priming in cold and draughty conditions. Make sure that there are no naked lights nearby when priming or filling.

Stripping with a paint remover is simpler but a much lengthier operation. The liquid should be generously applied and allowed to remain until the paint wrinkles and softens. Scraping follows to remove the film. With thick coatings several applications and subsequent scrapings are necessary. Following the stripping the work must be rinsed with either white spirit or water according to the type of stripper used. Directions will be on the can. All removers incorporate a waxy substance to prevent rapid evaporation of the solvent, and failure to eliminate would harm the new paint.

A cabinet maker's steel scraper is an excellent tool for stripping. Properly carried out, little rubbing down should be necessary, though the use of water may raise the grain somewhat, and ample time must be allowed for this to dry out. Priming is then carried out as for new work, adjusting the primer if necessary with only just enough thinners to ensure penetration. Over-thinning would result in an underbound primer, and too thick an application would drag and lie on the surface with consequent poor adhesion. Again everything depends on the foundation being secure. Badly charred wood must be removed, even if this means subsequent filling. On non-absorbent surfaces an aluminium primer may be more successful than a primer which depends on penetration alone.

Stopping

When the priming is dry, a light rub down is followed by the process of stopping the holes, and levelling small depressions and indentations. Any protruding nail heads should be punched in and defective timber replaced. Stopping material may be plain linseed oil putty, but, as this consists of nothing more than whiting ground in linseed oil, its strength is relatively poor. The addition of about 10 per cent white lead and a little red lead and gold size to putty makes what is known as hard stopping, and is greatly superior to the plain putty. If the mix is too sticky, a little added dry powdered whiting will rectify, if too dry, a little goldsize will restore plasticity. Strength may be increased by adding more pigment, red lead for hardening, and white lead for increased elasticity.

The stopping should be well pressed home into the indentations, taking care that it excludes any trapped air. Minute holes are difficult in this respect and may well be slightly enlarged with a small bradawl. The putty knife should be used, not only to press the material well home, but also to finally level the surface off to the surrounding work. As the red and white lead are very poisonous, the stopping should be placed on a small palette or putty board, a flat piece of ply about 4 in. square with a handle being very suitable as in

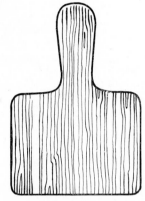

Fig. 4. PUTTY BOARD CUT FROM A SHEET OF PLYWOOD.

Fig. 4. Failing this a stripping knife may be used. Never use hard stopping from the palm of the hand. Stoppings may be coloured to match the priming or ground colour, using appropriate pigments, black for grey, ochre for cream, umber for brown, etc. Grey stopping looks better over aluminium priming if left for any time, but it is better to follow up with undercoating before the material has got too hard, as while this is still slightly plastic the brush can assist somewhat in levelling off slight protuberances inadvertently left.

Filling

Sometimes the surface after priming is uneven or the grain may be raised owing to exposure. To remedy this, filling has to be undertaken. Two types of filler are available, water mixed, rather in the nature of plaster, or oil or japan bound, having the consistency of rather liquid putty. Both are spread as evenly as possible over the whole surface with a filling knife, a flexible stripping knife with a true edge, using a stiff brush for mouldings with a little thinner material. When dry, the filled surface should be coated with a guide coat of thin dark grey or black in turps.

When in turn, this is dry, the whole is rubbed down with fine to medium glasspaper mounted on a rubbing block until the guide coat disappears, leaving a true and level surface. Traces of guide coat remaining reveal hollows, indicating the necessity for further filling. The rubbing down on oil-bound filler should be with water as a lubricant. Water mixed fillers are rubbed down dry. Always mount the glasspaper on a block to preserve a flat, true surface. Fillers by their nature are rather absorbent and should be coated with a 'long oil', i.e. rather oily undercoat, thus creating a suction-free base for subsequent coats. Without this oiling out, as it is called, normal undercoats would lose their binder into the filling and the pigment would lie on the top as a loosely adhering chalky film.

Manufactured woods such as chipboard and hardboard are best primed with an alkyd varnish sealer, specially made for the purpose by many firms. This seals the pores and tends to prevent subsequent rising of the fibres. The excessive suction of most hardboards makes the pigment gather in unsightly ridges when using a normal primer. Insulation boards benefit from a thin coat of glue size before priming. This and when painting lining paper are the only instances when preliminary sizing is permissible under an oil paint system. Size is strongly contractile, varying in volume according to humidity, eventually cracking superimposed paint.

New plaster and cement must be perfectly dry before painting, and, as these materials are usually basic chemically, they must be treated with a special alkali resist primer. The application of an ordinary oil paint would result in saponification, the whole turning to a brown sticky, soapy mess, especially in the presence of moisture. One exception is Keene's cement, the accepted practice being to follow the trowel. Directly the Keene's is hard enough to resist brush marks, a coat of sharp white lead is applied. The theory is that this prevents the hard marble-like film of crystals developing on the surface which would prevent adhesion. This does not mean that further coats can immediately follow.

The plaster must now be allowed to dry out thoroughly, which may take weeks or months. By this time the thin, turpsy white lead will have almost disappeared and any loose powder may be dusted from the surface before priming again. Before applying any primer the plaster or cement should be lightly rubbed with glasspaper and any making good and stopping done with similar material to the original, allowing ample time to dry. Asbestos sheeting is strongly alkaline and should receive two coats of resistant primer, as should also cement rendered walls.

Old painted plaster should be washed and rubbed down with sugar soap in the same way as for woodwork. Old distemper, limewash, and the like should be removed as much as possible by scrubbing and scraping, treating any large areas of making good as for new plaster.

Ferrous Metal

Iron and steel present special problems. With new iron, all foundry scale must be removed by scraping and wirebrushing. On large scale work a flame process should be employed. All traces of rust must be removed by chipping, scraping, and wirebrushing. Special chemicals are available to assist removal. Often these contain phosphoric acid which deposits an adherent film of iron phosphate which is receptive to paint. When the metal is dry, clean, and bright it must be primed immediately before further rusting occurs. Many primers are available and should be used as directed. New galvanized iron and zinc refuse to accept paint and must first be treated with a mordant solution, which, after its application has dulled the metal, is usually rinsed off, though some solutions may remain on. Follow the maker's directions implicitly. It is claimed that Calcium plumbate primer may be applied directly to galvanized iron and zinc with no previous mordant, a decided advantage when dealing with galvanized steel sashes. If possible, six months weathering is the best treatment if painting can be deferred so long. All metals should be degreased with white spirit before priming, and the smooth shiny surfaces of copper and aluminium etched with emery cloth.

SUGGESTED PRIMINGS

Soft Wood	*Red and White Lead*
Resinous Wood	*Aluminium Primer (Not Paint)*
Hard Wood	*Red and White Lead Long Oil*
Iron and Steel	*Red Lead, Zinc Chromate, Metallic Lead, Zinc Dust Paint, Calcium Plumbate*
Steel Sashes ⎫ Galvanized Iron ⎬	*Calcium Plumbate*
Aluminium	*Zinc Chromate*
Copper	*Alkyd Resin Varnish Pigmented with Aluminium*
Plaster and Cement ⎫ Asbestos ⎬	*Alkali Resistant Primer*
Hardboard	*Alkyd Resin Varnish or Sealer*
Insulating Board	*Thin Size then Normal Wood Primer*

When using a particular brand of paint, either from choice or to a specification, it is advisable to prime, undercoat, and finish with the one firm's products throughout. Their chemists and technicians have devised a system of successive coatings which are compatible. An excellent priming made by A, followed by filling made by B, equally excellent undercoatings by C, and finish coats with D's superb gloss paint will not combine the perfections of all, and failure is more than a probability.

3 External Painting

THE FOREGOING chapter having dealt with the preparation and priming of various surfaces, the actual procedure of outside painting may be described as if working to an actual specification for the external painting of a normal house, dealing with the various sections progressively. The same basic principles apply to most jobs, although requirements for plant and equipment will vary widely. The following model specification, applies to re-painting, but new work requires the same thorough treatment.

Fig. 1. TWO MEN RAISING LADDER FROM GROUND.

Gutters, Inside and Out, Stackpipes, and All Ironwork

Thoroughly scrape and wirebrush to remove all scale and rust, degrease, spot prime, and paint two coats undercoat and one coat hard gloss enamel paint (make or quality stipulated).

This is the first operation to consider, as all external work should commence at the top, so that dirt and dust cannot fall on completed lower work. Scraping and wirebrushing must be systematic, thorough cleaning being absolutely essential. In towns it is advisable to rinse the work with white spirit, drying off with clean rag or cotton waste. Deposits of greasy soot, diesel oil, etc., lessens adhesion and sometimes prevents the drying of the paint. Gutters must be thoroughly clean and dry inside and any defects remedied by the plumber. Take the first opportunity to paint the insides. With our fickle climate days may elapse once an opportunity has been missed. For cheaper work, two coats of bitumastic may be used inside, or, better, rust-resisting primer and one coat oil paint. All rusted and bare work should then be touched up with rust inhibiting paint (spot primed) and allowed to dry. Painting can proceed as specified, following implicitly the maker's directions as to thinning and application. Never paint in damp or foggy weather or in low temperatures.

If the soffit and fascia boards are, as often, finished in a lighter colour than the gutter, these should be prepared at the same time as the gutter and painted first and the darker colour to the ironwork cut in after. For preliminary work the ladder should reach over the gutter unless an easy reach stay is used, so that the inside is visible without dangerous reaching back. Finishing face work is best undertaken by using the stay or with the ladder placed underneath. If right handed, work from right to left, this applies to all painted work and a trial will prove that this provides maximum comfort and efficiency. When working at a height never reach too far, and make sure that scaffold is always secure. For bridging over wide windows, cripples and planks may be required (Fig. 2).

When working above the gutter, such as to dormer windows, etc., the ladder should be tied to a stout screw eye securely fixed in the soffit board; with modern asbestos soffits, make sure of a timber fixing which is usually revealed by the nail heads. A sack of straw should be placed on the roof at the head of the ladder, and the necessary ladder or steps laid on this to provide access to the work above. Another sack of 'softening' is placed under the top. The weight of a man standing at the top of the ladder while the other is working on the roof above is an added and sometimes necessary, precaution.

Fig. 2. BOARD RESTING ON CRIPPLES FITTED TO TWO LADDERS.
Note that the arrangement shown does not comply with safety regulations,
the cripples should have been extended so that the two planks lie side by
side, making the platform twice the width.

WOODWORK

Fascias, Soffits, Bargeboards, Sashes and Frames, Gates and Posts

Burn off all blistered and scored work, rub down, twice knot, prime and stop, and paint an extra undercoat. For the remainder, thoroughly degrease, scrape, and rub down. Twice apply knotting to exposed knots, patch-prime all bare work, and stop. Hack off any loose putties, patch prime, and make good with white lead putty. Paint the whole with two undercoats and one coat hard gloss enamel paint (make or quality stipulated).

Carry out the preparation and priming as described in the previous chapter. Work should again commence at the top, and, as a precaution against inclement weather, sheltered work under porches and covered ways should be deferred until the exposed work is brought forward, or rain intervenes. At the same time, do not delay this protected work to such an extent that extra journeys and the retention of plant are necessary to complete.

Wide groups of casement sashes are often best dealt with by the use of planks on cripples (Fig. 2), otherwise securely fixed ladders of appropriate height should be used. A comfortable scaffold is necessary for burning off, which should only be undertaken from positions where there is a minimum danger to the worker from falling hot paint.

Sashes

When painting cased framed sashes a regular sequence should be observed. First reverse the sashes, top to bottom and bottom to top, and deal with the exposed upper portions of the bottom sash, following with the top external beads and frame and the top edge of the top sash. Raise the latter a little and complete, and push right up. The bottom sash is then pulled down and completed. Finally complete the runners and frame and sill. Pull the top sash down a little and the bottom sash up, touch up if necessary, and leave open to dry. The arrangement is shown in Fig. 3.

Special care should be taken with the joint between the wood and brick or stone cill. First rake out thoroughly and when painting, extend the cutting in over the lower cill about half an inch to provide a key for the subsequent stopping which should be well worked in when the paint is dry. This stopping should be, of course, protected with further coats of paint. In cases of actual damp penetration a mastic should be used. Notes should be taken during the preparatory stages of defects requiring the attention of the carpenter or glazier.

Re-glazing

Glazing is often carried out by the painter and the procedure is simple. To remove old glass, the face putties are removed with a hacking knife (Fig. 4) held at a suitable angle and tapped with a hammer, removing brads with pincers. When putties are cleared, the glass must be carefully removed, a tap or two from behind sometimes assisting. Next the bed putties must be hacked

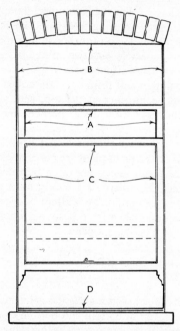

Fig. 3. ORDER OF PAINTING SASHES FROM OUTSIDE   1. Place in position shown. 2. Paint what is seen of lower sash (A). 3. Paint top half of frame (B).   4. Paint top sash (C).   5. Paint sill (D).   6. Close sashes to within 1 in. 7. Complete painting.

out to the rebate, which must be left perfectly clean and smooth. Next prime the rebate and allow to dry. If in a hurry to re-glaze, knot instead of prime. It is necessary to stop suction with one or the other, otherwise oil would be absorbed from the putty.

Measure accurately for the new glass, allowing $\frac{1}{8}$ in. less than the actual size and making proper allowance for the top rebate of lower cased framed sashes. When the glass has been cut, try it for size and then place safely aside. With soft, not sticky putty, press in a bed with the fingers, allowing a good ¼ in. thickness all round the rebates. Reject any hard lumps in the putty. These are obvious when the fingers are used.

When the bedding is complete, place the glass in position by gently pushing with the fingers progressively round the edges, using both hands on opposite sides. When the glass is tightly bedded, shown by the squeezing out of the back putty, it should be secured by carefully bradding in. Small squares require one brad in the middle of each side; larger ones need brads at intervals of 12 in. or so. Tap the brads in with the back of the hacking knife or a small hammer, keeping the tool flat on the glass during use to minimise risk of breakage.

The face putties are next spread and evened to smooth chamfer with the putty knife (Fig. 5), care being taken that the edge is about ⅛ in. less than

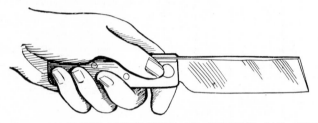

Fig. 4. HACKING KNIFE USED TO REMOVE OLD PUTTY.

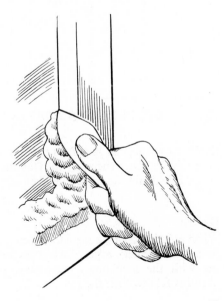

Fig. 5. STRIKING OFF GLAZING PUTTY. The putty is squeezed out, not sliced. It helps to dampen the knife beforehand.

the depth of the rebate, ensuring that when the paint is cut in slightly over the glass, it does not show from the inside. Damping the blade of the putty knife assists it to slide smoothly in the final levelling strokes. The excess back putty is removed by running the knife round the inside of the rebates.

Odd shapes require the cutting of a templet in stout paper or cardboard. For beaded glazing, remove the beads carefully and number in order for replacement. Bed in the glass with putty before refixing beads. For steel sashes a special mastic putty should be used, as ordinary putty wrinkles with the expansion and contraction of the metal. Sheet glass is made in varying

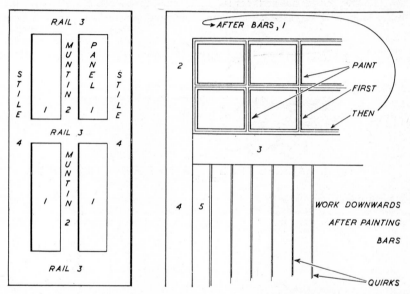

Fig. 6. ORDER IN PAINTING PARTS OF ROOM AND GARAGE DOOR.

thicknesses expressed as ounces to the square foot; e.g., 26 oz., 32 oz.; plate glass in thicknesses such as $\frac{1}{4}$ in. Obscured and decorated glass is known by name. If in doubt, a sample should be taken when ordering.

Doors

When painting doors, a regular sequence should be observed. First paint the frame, and the edge exposed when opened. Next come the panels, commencing with the mouldings, completing panels, and laying off mouldings. Muntins follow, then the rails, and finally the stiles (Fig. 6). This sequence

Fig. 7. CUTTING-IN WHEN PAINTING. The brush is held in line with the direction of the stroke.

Fig. 8 (*below*). ALTERNATIVE METHOD OF CUTTING-IN.

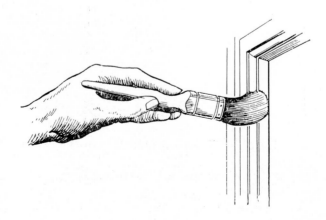

ensures that all crossing brushwork is eliminated. This is the traditional method, though with modern quick-setting paints, it is often better to commence at the top, working progressively downwards, observing the

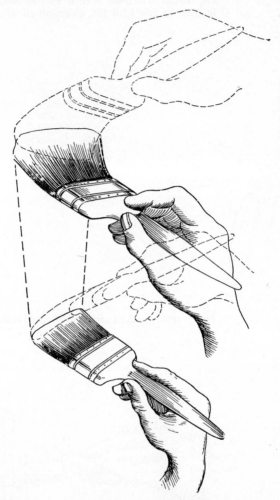

Fig. 9. HANDLING BRUSH WHEN SPREADING PAINT.

sequence of panel, muntin, rail, and stile as far as possible, and maintaining a wet edge continuously.

When painting garage doors or similar glazed work, cut in the inner bars

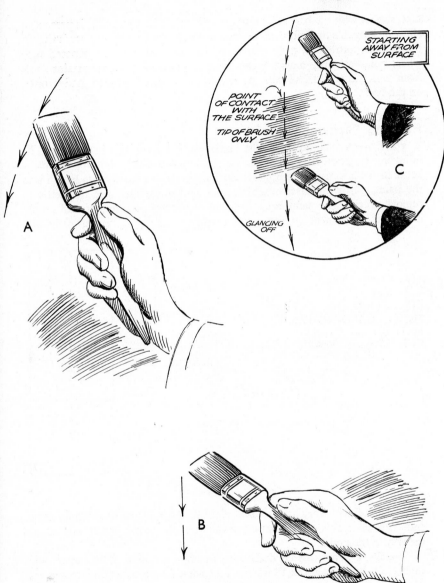

Fig. 10. HOW BRUSH IS HANDLED WHEN LAYING-OFF PAINT. The brush glides on to and off the surface. It is never dabbed abruptly on the work.

first, so that with the bars adjoining the rails and stiles a wet edge is present to allow picking this up before set. Garage and all doors opening outwards should be painted both sides, particular attention being paid to the exposed tops where penetration by moisture can cause severe damage. If rust stains show from under hinges, these must be removed, de-rusted, primed, and painted on the back.

Painting Technique

A good brush technique should be attempted from the beginning. The following suggestions are for the right handed worker. Holding the paint kettle in the left hand, the brush is dipped for about a third of its length into the paint, partly withdrawn, and tapped against the inside of the kettle to remove excess. The paint is applied first at the top right and spread evenly in all directions, next up and down, then horizontally, again vertically, and

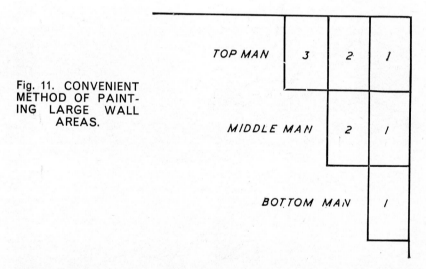

Fig. 11. CONVENIENT METHOD OF PAINTING LARGE WALL AREAS.

finally laid off with very light strokes, right through, lifting away gently at the end. Vertical in this context means in the direction of the panel, rail, etc., or the way of the grain.

Usually a panel can be dealt with in one operation. With larger units such as flush doors, about 18 in. at a time should be brushed in, crossed and laid off, then the next portion completed and laid off into the preceding, and so on to the extremity. Skirtings, fascias, etc., are dealt with by working progressively along the length, always working into and not away from the completed sections. Brush work should always follow the structural direction.

Wall surfaces used to be laid off vertically, but with modern semi-gloss and lustre finishes, even laying off in all directions often gives the best results. Paint should be spread with a flowing motion, avoiding excess which would cause runs and curtaining, at the same time avoiding rubbing out too much and starving the film.

Cutting In

Cutting in is the expression used to describe the operation of working to a line or edge, such as glass (Figs. 7 and 8). This is best performed by generously charging but not overloading the brush, which should be laid obliquely and long ways against the work. With a steady, continuous stroke wet the surface as far as the brushful will allow. This preliminary stroke seldom covers the whole surface, little misses occur, but assists the succeeding strokes which are carried out in reversing directions with a little less colour in the brush until satisfactorily completed.

The brush in its progress should push a little droplet of colour ahead lubricating its passage, the sole purpose of the first bold stroke. Tentative dabs are useless and a good straight clean line can only be achieved with long confident strokes. Holding the brush into awkward corners and shaking it without withdrawing forces the paint into the crevices without spoiling adjoining surfaces. For sash cutting, a $\frac{3}{4}$ in. or 1 in. brush which has been worn to a bevel edge is best. Using the brush edgeways increases the effective resistance of the bristles to spread and facilitates control. For all work use the largest size brush compatible with the type of paint and surface. Stiff paints require shorter and narrower brushes than thin, easy-flowing mixtures. Care should be taken that runs do not occur from the bases of mouldings, quirks, etc., impinging on rails underneath. A few minutes after application the work should be examined and any runs removed before it is too late.

Large Surfaces

Painting large wall surfaces is best achieved from an independent scaffold. If done from ladders, some thought is necessary before commencement. Generally it is best for one man to commence at the top right and when he moves to the next shift, another follows with a shorter ladder completing the section immediately under the first while the other completes the next top section. Both then move again to the right, to be followed by a third painter at the next lower level and so on, thus maintaining easily worked wet edges, and an even progression. Fig. 11 shows the idea. At the extreme end of the wall each successive ladder is lowered a little to allow for completion. Extension ladders are the most suitable for use in this way. Intervening obstructions such as windows may present problems which should be solved before commencing.

All scaffolding regulations must be rigidly observed. To engage the attention of a painter working above it is usual to signal by tapping the side of the ladder. The safest way to raise or lower a ladder is for the heaviest man to stand on the bottom rung, grasping the third rung and extending the body rearwards thus acting as a counter balance while another raises the ladder by pushing up the sides as in Fig. 1. When ascending or descending a ladder, grasp the sides, not the rungs, if one breaks there is still something to hold on to. All ladders should be secured at the top and when used on slippery surfaces should be footed by a man standing on the bottom rung. This is especially important on pavements to give warning to and avoid impact from passers by. Carrying a long ladder upright is accomplished by resting a side against the shoulder and grasping alternate rungs with the hands, the upper pushing down and the lower pulling up to maintain the vertical when lifted a little off the ground. In the event of swaying or loss of control, firmly place the foot of the ladder on the ground, this should immediately steady it. Manoeuvres with long ladders in high winds are dangerous and should be avoided. Always make sure that securing cords to steps are sound and that they are properly extended and that trestles are secure and level. Wood blocks and folding wedges are useful for this purpose.

The application of Snowcem is usually undertaken with a distempering technique, and the actual work should be planned as mentioned for oil paint; similarly with plastic emulsions and distempers. Special outside-qualities of these latter are obtainable. Beware of water paints on 'stucco or rough-cast walls above brickwork which may eventually be discoloured by streaks of whitish material when weathering has brought about eventual disintegration. To guard against this all thinning of distempers should be with petrifying liquid and emulsions with special medium usually supplied for this purpose, but sooner or later breakdown of any water paint is inevitable.

Special finishing techniques are dealt with in later chapters.

4 Internal Painting

INTERIOR DECORATING has now achieved almost the status of a profession, unfortunately often practised by people who have little or no practical knowledge and experience. It is apparently sufficient that these exotic interior decorators can impose on a gullible clientele bizarre schemes designated with the sacred catchword 'contemporary', durability and suitability for purpose being almost completely ignored. Good design and décor must be based on good technique and practical experience.

Preparation

Before commencing any work, all movable furniture, curtains, fittings, and floor coverings should be removed. If, however, some has to remain, this should be placed as conveniently as possible and completely covered with dust sheets. These may be of cotton, twill, or polythene. These latter are completely waterproof, but rather easily torn. Curtain runners should be removed and stored in a safe place. It is often a good practice when removing fittings to return the screws only into their original positions, thus avoiding loss or mixing up. Remove door furniture, refixing handles without the roses, or, better still, replace temporarily with old ones if available until all is complete.

The normal room redecorations require two pairs of steps or trestles of suitable height, planks of sufficient length, pasteboards, pails, brushes, kettles, hawk, etc. Some pasteboards are reversible and turned upside down form a good bench for paint mixing, etc., Following the procedure of the previous chapter is a model specification for complete redecorations to a living-room.

Ceiling, Cornice, and Frieze. Wash off, stop, and distemper two coats.
Walls. Strip, stop, and distemper two coats.
Woodwork. Wash and rub down, touch up, stop and paint two coats undercoat and one coat hard gloss paint.

Work should always commence at the top and away from the light. Place the steps and plank at and parallel to, the window side about two feet from the wall. Begin by thoroughly and evenly wetting in the whole of the ceiling, cornice, and frieze within reach, using preferably warm water applied with a wash-down or worn distemper brush. This will probably soak in and the wetting should be repeated if necessary.

Next, a worn brush should be used in an oblique scrubbing motion, holding the brush at about an angle of 20 degrees to the ceiling. If the existing distemper is size bound, this scrubbing will loosen and remove the coating and the scrubbing should be persevered with until the plaster is exposed. A final rinsing with the brush, followed by a sponge or flannel should ensure a completely clean surface. This is absolutely essential, as any residue of soft distemper might easily cause subsequent flaking.

If, however, the existing decoration is oil-bound or washable distemper, plastic emulsion, or other paint, removal will not be possible, and in this case washing and drying off will have to be confined to removal of surface dirt, making sure that no loosely adhering material remains. Scraping may have to be undertaken, rubbing down the edges and if necessary levelled by filling.

SECTION OF PLASTER

V-SHAPED INCISION

Fig. 1. HOW PLASTER IS UNDERCUT.

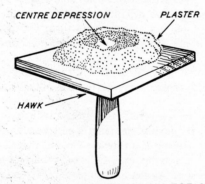

Fig. 2. PLASTER PLACED ON HAWK FOR MIXING.

Any cracks should be cut out to a V-shaped or undercut incision as in Fig. 1, thoroughly wetted by vigorously splashing with the wash-down brush, and stopped in with either a proprietary filler or Keene's cement. Small quantities are best prepared by making a heap of the dry filler or plaster on a hawk, making a centre depression, and filling this with cold water. With the trowel or stopping knife the outside of the heap is transferred to the pool in the centre until all is mixed to a plastic state as in Fig. 2. With the aid of a small trowel or filling knife the plaster should be pressed firmly into the cracks or holes and levelled off, excess surrounding the crack being removed with the edge of the wet brush and finally trowelled level. The V cut ensures that even if the filling shrinks slightly it cannot fall out.

With modern plaster board ceilings the raking out must be carefully under-

Fig. 3. PREPARING THE WALLS—CRACKS BEING MADE GOOD.

taken as the hessian or scrym originally applied over the joints may be disturbed. A minimum amount of cutting out should be sufficient if a good proprietary filler or cellulose filler is employed. Always make sure that the cracks or holes are thoroughly damp before filling. Plaster sets by chemical combination with the mixing water and if this is absorbed by suction from dry surfaces, it may easily return to something like its original powdered state.

Removing Old Paper

The correct sequence in preparation should be observed, and before proceeding further with the ceiling after complete washing off, the walls should be stripped. Thoroughly soak the whole surface with warm water, repeating this until penetration to the plaster is complete. Special powders are available which, when dissolved in the warm water, materially assist in the soaking of difficult papers, many layers of which may be present. Varnish or other papers with an impervious surface require the removal of the protective coating with a water-soluble paint remover, care being taken to protect paint work or floor coverings. When the varnish, etc., has been removed, stripping proceeds in the normal way. Scoring diagonally with a knife through the paper but not the plaster assists in penetration of water.

Sometimes old painted relief papers are best removed dry, a laborious undertaking at the best and in extreme cases, necessitating the wholesale re-plastering of the ceiling or wall. The stripping knife should be tried at all angles. Sometimes a tough paper will strip easier upwards, sometimes downwards, or sideways. Once a start has been made, try and keep the knife at a slight angle on the plaster, thus avoiding digging in. With very difficult papers of all kinds use only about half the width of the knife under the paper and so halve the effort. Never allow paper that has once been damped to dry out as this often makes it doubly difficult to remove. The paste seems to be reactivated and repellent to subsequent penetration by water.

Cleaning Down

After the paper has been removed, the walls should be thoroughly scrubbed with clean water to remove any remaining traces of paper, size, and paste, scraping again if necessary. Any adhering waste should be scrubbed from skirtings and floor margins. Pay particular attention to the edges of switch blocks and similar projections. Nothing annoys the paperhanger more than encountering odd residues of paper where he wishes to make a clean cut.

While the walls are still damp, the making good and stopping should be carried out, again cutting out as previously described. Large holes should be cut back to clean non-friable and firm edges and all loose material removed back to the brick. These larger holes are best made good with 1–3 cement and sand, brought to a level surface about $\frac{1}{4}$ in. bare of the surrounding plaster, well scored in criss-cross grooves to provide a key and when set, skimmed with Keene's cement or other suitable wall plaster. Plaster alone to a depth of an inch or more would take much longer to dry out.

All edges to architraves and skirtings must be stopped, as nothing looks worse than the dark line of a crack showing at the junction of a light wall paper and paint. Sometimes difficulty arises where the wall ends at the skirting, attempts to fill merely resulting in the plaster falling down the gap. Damp paper screwed up to a suitable thickness, pushed into the gap, and well wedged so that it is just below the top of the skirting will allow stopping to proceed. Still better, make a papier mache by mixing the paper with dilute plaster instead of water.

Sizing

When the walls are dry, they should be lightly glasspapered and sized if to be papered. As our specification stipulates distemper, sizing must be omitted. On no account should the application of size precede distemper. Assuming for the time being that we are papering the room, the size should be prepared by placing a ¼ lb. concentrated size powder in a pail and mixed to a thin cream with a little tepid water. This will soon form a gelatinous mass to which should be added half-a-gallon of boiling water, stirring in vigorously.

The size should be applied generously and evenly with a distemper brush while still hot, further hot water being added if necessary to dilute further. Depending on the quality, a quarter-of-a-pound of size is usually sufficient to make a gallon or more. Never use too thick, its sole purpose is to provide even porosity, not to entirely stop suction. It is often better to allow a few seconds for the water to come off the boil before mixing. On cooling the size will become a jelly which can be easily liquefied by heating.

Tub size is supplied in kegs and only requires the addition of hot water. Cold water sizes are also available but are seldom as strong as the hot water variety. Sizing should be followed with further glasspapering. When using cellulose pastes, size with a dilute solution of the paste. These pastes have a solvent and lifting action on ordinary size.

Distemper

The paintwork must now be prepared as described in Chapter 2 and the room is then ready for its decorations. Commencing with the ceiling, the first coat of distemper should be applied. If washable distemper or oil-bound water paint is employed, start by erecting the scaffold as for washing off, again working from the light.

Two pails should be available, one containing water. Place about 4 lb. of distemper in the other, taking care to scrape down the sides of the keg after abstracting, and levelling off the top. Before adding any thinnings, beat up the distemper, and then add water to obtain a creamy consistency. Failure to beat up first sometimes causes a lumpy mix which can only be broken up by straining. With 'hot', i.e. very absorbent, plasters it may be advantageous to add petrifying liquid and water in equal proportions. A trial should be made and if the mix spreads and obliterates reasonably well, no further adjustment is needed.

Lay the distemper on freely and evenly in all directions, working in straight strips parallel to the wall about eighteen inches wide. Maintain a wet edge so that, when the next section is brushed in, the distemper flows evenly into that already completed, and so on systematically across the whole ceiling. Failure to maintain a wet edge results in a double thickness of distemper at the joins. This overlapping casts shadows and presents the appearance of dark streaks, accentuated by the extra whiteness of the two thicknesses. Technically these overlaps are known as flashes or catches. Working away from the light obviates this to a limited extent, the light falling against the ridges. Light falling across them will obviously cause a cast shadow. Move the

Fig. 4. HOW DISTEMPER BRUSH IS HELD.

scaffold quickly when a shift is completed and immediately brush along the whole of the edge to liven it up. It is at moves where catches are most likely to occur. Always proceed methodically. Never attempt to re-touch distemper that is partly set, and examine closely for misses as work progresses.

With an average size ceiling, two men should be sufficient, working with a pail between them. With larger areas more should be available so that each man can deal with a section about eight feet wide. This necessitates larger quantities and more pails, and should be 'boxed' by pouring from pail to pail until all are of the same consistency. For very large ceilings use a running scaffold or a patent staging to minimize time in moving.

Allow at least twenty-four hours for drying before applying the next coat, using the same technique. All spots must be immediately wiped up from floors and paintwork. If sufficient sheets are available, cover the floor beforehand, or alternatively, damp the whole floor to prevent absorption and consequent rapid drying of splashes. Do not make it wet enough to be slippery.

The technique employed with plastic emulsion paints is similar, except that a priming coat thinned with fifty per cent water ensures penetration and is followed by two normal coats. Some makers supply a transparent medium which acts as a binder and provides a certain amount of sheen. Use strictly in accordance with directions. Plastic emulsions may be re-coated immediately they are dry, a definite advantage. They are considered safe to use over new plaster which has had a reasonable time to dry out. They should not be used where condensation is prevalent, as in kitchens or bathrooms. Although perhaps successful on drying walls, never where damp is active.

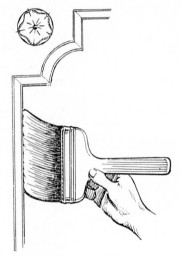

Fig. 5. CUTTING-IN WITH DISTEMPER BRUSH.

Soft Distempers

Soft or size-bound distempers are applied over a preliminary sealing preparation known as claircolle or clearcole. This is prepared by thinning the distemper with about 50 per cent size. The mixture is applied freely, and, when dry, coated with the distemper suitably thinned with water only. Never attempt to apply two coats of soft distemper. The second will loosen the first, resulting in patchiness and catches.

Size-bound distempers are rather transparent when wet but become opaque and much lighter in colour when dry. They are comparatively cheap and durable in positions that cannot be rubbed, and can be easily and

51

completely removed when necessary. There is much to be said for this quality, as it is obvious that any subsequent form of decoration is much more likely to succeed over a virgin surface.

Preparing Distempers

For those who wish to prepare their own distemper the procedure is as follows. First, three-parts fill a pail with cold water and then fill nearly to the top with lumps of whiting until the water reaches the brim. Leave for some hours to soak and then pour off all excess water which should have cleared. Now prepare $\frac{1}{2}$ lb. concentrated size with about a quart of boiling water, stir, and when properly melted, pour into the whiting, first stirring in with a stick.

With sleeves rolled up, thoroughly mix and knead with the hands until all is almagamated. If a soft, off-white is required, the mixture after straining and cooling will be ready for use. It should possess a jelly-like consistency which spreads easily when suitably thinned with plain water. Extra size may be added to make the first coating claircolle.

If a dead white is required, mix a little dry lime or ultramarine blue with water to a thin cream, and add to the whiting until a pale blue results. This will dry out a dead or cold white with extra obliterative powers. If a cream is required use dry ochre in the same way. Other tints may be obtained by using suitable pigments such as dry lime green, yellow, red, umber, etc. The distemper always dries much lighter, and, to match a colour, a sample should be painted on to a piece of lining paper, and dried over heat to reveal the eventual colour. A great deal of judgement is required and it is advisable to work gradually, making successive additions of stainers and trials until the desired hue is attained.

Experienced craftsmen still maintain that this home-made whitewash is the best obtainable. The proportion of size to pigment can be widely varied according to differing conditions. Unless a little preservative is added, putrefaction of the size soon takes place in hot weather, rendering the material useless, consequently only enough should be mixed to last a few days.

Distempering has been dealt with at some length because it is of the utmost importance. A poor ceiling can mar the appearance of an otherwise attractive room. Good distempering is a measure of the craftsman's competence and real aesthetic pleasure can arise from merely looking at a fine matt surface created by good technique. On any but the finest of surfaces the best results can only be achieved by first hanging a lining paper as later described. Distempering over lining paper is easy, one coat of soft distemper often sufficing, but care must be taken to avoid misses as the uncovered parts of the lining paper eventually turn brown.

On old ceilings it is common practice to use washable distemper or emulsion paint to save stripping when redecoration becomes necessary. A well lined ceiling may sometimes be sponged off, however, claircolled and re-distempered. For first-class work the lining paper may be sized and painted one coat of flat white prior to any finishing decoration, thus ensuring permanence of the lining.

Distempering Walls

When distempering walls the same principles should be observed, taking particular care to maintain wet edges and avoid catches. Long flank walls are best dealt with by one man commencing at a top corner nearest the source of light, brushing in a shift about half-way down, and carrying on with adjoining shifts, while the second man completes to the skirting, following right through. In this way a comparatively short edge is left at any time. Large areas such as staircases require special planning and all necessary scaffold should be in place at the start.

Old flaking surfaces are often encountered which defy complete removal. When all loose material has been removed all hollows should be flushed up with a cellulose or plaster filler, using the broad or filling knife. Often the best results are obtained by leaving the surface a little proud, and rubbing down with glasspaper mounted on a rubbing block when dry. The filling should be spot primed and the whole coated with a sealer primer. This sealer should penetrate and bind the old material, converting old distemper to a sort of oil paint. Distemper can then be applied in the normal manner.

It is often found that old cornices are stained and flaking. The application of a sealer primer is a useful way of renovating what may otherwise prove to be an unsightly blemish. Sealer coats may have to be lightly scuffed with glasspaper before applying distemper, otherwise cissing may occur. Cissing is the term used to describe the separation of the water paint into tiny globules and is evidence that the somewhat oily primer is refusing to accept the water paint. Plastic emulsions are particularly liable to ciss.

A similar procedure should be observed when using paint in lieu of distemper. Many delightful effects are obtained with flat, eggshell, and semi-gloss paints, many of which are applied coat on coat with no separate undercoat. Some of these paints are thixotropic, i.e. in the form of a jelly. They should not be thinned or stirred, as the friction involved in spreading temporarily liquefies the medium, ensuring easy application. Its gelatinous structure prevents splashes and drips. When painting over lining paper, first apply a weak coat of size. This avoids undue suction and prevents the linseed oil chemically attacking the paper. The oil also darkens paper and thus robs a light paint of hiding power.

If the ceilings and walls of bathrooms and kitchens are in such bad order that lining is necessary, sizing and painting the lining paper will ensure that moisture penetration cannot take place, providing a steam resistant coating

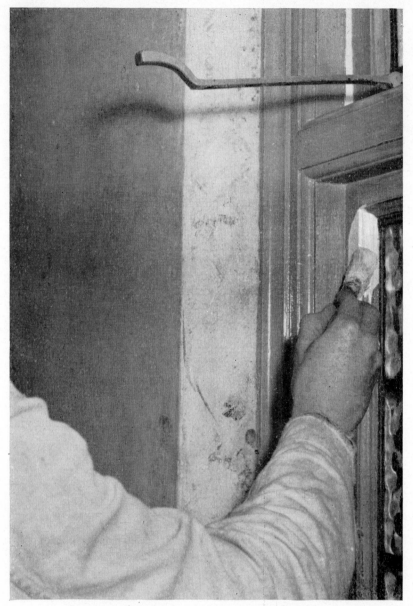

Fig. 6. PAINTING MOULDING OF WINDOW SASH.

is used. Condensation is a great enemy of paint and steps should be taken to ensure that none is present when painting, or likely to occur before drying. A microscopically thin film of moisture may not be apparent to sight or touch, but its imprisonment between layers of paint could be disastrous, causing flaking and peeling. Condensation settling on freshly applied paint causes blooming and destroys gloss and depth of colour.

To return rather belatedly to our specification (page 45), the general principles of painting described in the previous chapter should be followed. With distempered walls, painting is completed last; when papering, at least the edges should be finished so that cutting in is avoided. Oil from paint would be sucked up by the paper, forming a dark stain. If painting after papering is unavoidable, a thin coat of size should be applied about an inch deep all the way round against the paint work, to prevent absorption by the paper. When painting edges prior to papering, cut over on to the adjoining plaster for about half an inch or somewhat less. If the paper is inadvertently cut a little short in places the presence of the paint will often conceal the slight gap.

Window Frames

To paint a cased frame sash a reverse procedure to that of external painting is adopted. First reverse the sashes and complete the bottom of the top sash and the underside of the bottom sash rail. Reverse to proper positions and complete top sash and top rail of bottom sash. Next while on the steps, complete the runners, pulling out the sash cords with the hand to facilitate painting behind. Complete the top half of frame and architraves, descend, and complete to base. Complete the bottom sash and finally the cill or window board. Some painters complete the bottom sash before commencing the top, but there is the risk that dust may possibly settle on the new paint or it may become soiled from contact with clothing.

Doors

When painting a door, the edge showing into the room when opened should be painted first. If narrow edges are completed afterwards, some of the paint may creep round on to the face where it would be much more noticeable than on the edge. The frame should be painted as far as the return edge of the rebates to the top and lock side. The hanging edge and its rebate properly belong to the other side. There is some variation in practice between different localities, and the solution is, when in Rome do as Rome does. Similar difficulties arise with casement windows and doors. As a general principle paint that which is visible. Never paint the outside runners to a top case framed sash nor the inner runners to the bottom sash. These have most use and accumulations of paint would prevent free movement of the sliding sashes. It is sufficient to paint at top and bottom for about two inches, completing with a neat arc. Make sure that rebates are properly painted so that misses on the runners are not visible from the other side.

Special decorative effects will be discussed in later chapters, but the basis of these and indeed, all decoration is thorough preparation and good plain painting.

5 Paperhanging

THE ART OF paperhanging may be readily acquired by anyone prepared to work methodically and with extreme care and cleanliness. Beginners should practice first in rooms of little importance such as attics and cupboards. Although one may feel that such rooms do not merit top grade work, every endeavour should be made to use these opportunities to obtain as near perfection as possible.

Quantities
After the paper has been selected, the requisite quantity must be ascertained to avoid waste or shortage. The waste of time involved in obtaining an extra roll may cost more than the piece itself and the extra piece may have to come from another batch of a slightly different shade. Wallpaper manufacturers supply tables which state the number of pieces required for average rooms. These tables enable the paperhanger to see at a glance the number of rolls required, after he has ascertained the perimeter (distance round) and height

of the room. These tables are nearly always on the generous side, modern rooms often having windows and doors above the average in size and in these cases, accurate calculation may effect a saving. A typical table is given on page 157.

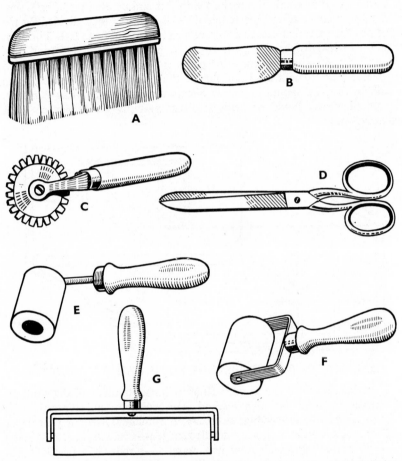

Fig. 1. TOOLS REQUIRED BY THE PAPERHANGER.   A. Brush.   B. Knife.
C. Casing Knife.   D. Scissors.   E and F. Seam rollers.   G. Roller.

English wallpaper is approximately $11\frac{1}{2}$ yds. long by 21 in. wide, and reputed to cover nearly 7 sq. yds. It would seem that to find the surface area of the walls by multiplying the perimeter by the height and converting this to square yards, dividing by 7 with an allowance of 10 per cent for waste should provide a reasonably accurate answer. With deductions allowed for doors, windows, and average height, this method is still not the best.

A Good System

A better way is to obtain the perimeter in feet and divide by $1\frac{3}{4}$ (feet), thus giving the number of lengths required. This figure is then divided by the number of lengths that can be cut from a roll. A wall 6 ft. to 6 ft. 6 in. high would cut 5 lengths per piece; 7 ft. to 7 ft. 6 in. 4 lengths; 8 ft. to 10 ft. 6 in. 3 lengths; and so on, using average patterns. When using this method the perimeter measurement need not include the small sections over doors and windows, as there should be ample offcuts to accommodate this filling in. Ample allowance should be made for large patterns which may cut with excessive waste.

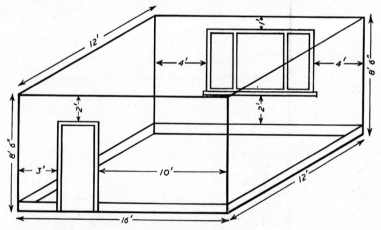

Fig. 2. DIAGRAMMATIC VIEW OF ROOM GIVING MAIN SIZES.

Paperhangers often use an odd roll of wallpaper to mark off the numbers of lengths required and this method is especially useful for staircases. Commencing at the top landing he counts off as follows. Assuming the paper will here cut 4 lengths, 1, 2, 3, 4—1 roll; 1, 2, 3, 4—2 rolls; 1, 2, 3, 4—3 rolls; 1, 2—3½ rolls; long length from half newel 1—4 rolls, 1, 2 (according to height of flank)—5 rolls; 1, 2, 3—6 rolls; 1, 2, 3—7 rolls. Flank now completed and on first landing, 1, 2, 3, 4—8 rolls, and so on right down the whole staircase. The inexperienced would have to measure the relative heights, but the practical paperhanger readily assesses the number of lengths required. In measuring, the greatest length from the rake of the string to the ceiling must be taken and due allowance made for waste in cutting and matching elaborate patterns.

Quantities for ceilings may be obtained similarly. A ceiling 13 ft. wide by 18 ft. long would require $10\frac{2}{7}$ lengths (18 divided by $1\frac{3}{4}$). Only 2 lengths could be cut from each piece, therefore 6 pieces would be required unless the last 6 in. were joined. Lining paper is 22 in. wide and 5 pieces would just be sufficient. Double rolls of lining paper are now obtainable. These often effect a great saving and whereas with these dimensions only 2 could be cut from a single piece, 5 would come from the double roll and this ceiling could be lined with 2 double rolls—a saving of 20 per cent.

Friezes are measured by length, bearing in mind that the maximum width must not exceed 21 in. or extra strips will be required. For widths up to $10\frac{1}{2}$ in (11 in. for lining paper) two widths may be cut from each length. Widths of 7 in. can be cut three to a roll.

The diagram in Fig. 2 demonstrates the application of the method to a room. The beginner may find that the preparation of a plan is helpful.

PERIMETER:

Window Wall	4 feet	plus	4 feet	8 feet
Side Walls	12 ,,	,,	12 ,,	24 ,,
Door Wall	3 ,,	,,	10 ,,	13 ,,
				45 feet

DIVIDE BY $1\frac{3}{4}$ feet

$$\frac{45 \times 4}{7} = 26 \text{ lengths.}$$

HEIGHT 8 ft. DIVIDE 34 ft. 6 in. by 8 = 4 lengths per roll.
DIVIDE 26 by 4 = $6\frac{1}{2}$ rolls.

The $\frac{1}{2}$-roll and offcuts should provide filling in over and under window and over door. For the sake of clarity, chimney breast has been omitted, the projection of this would probably require another 2 lengths, with possibly saving a little with short lengths over the fireplace, but little would be available for filling in. Seven pieces would be very close in this case, and the tables for a room this size state 8 pieces.

The ceiling being 16 ft. across would only allow 2 lengths to be cut from a roll, and 12 ft. divided by $1\frac{3}{4}$ (ft.) gives 7 lengths, therefore 4 rolls would be required, a number which agrees with the tables.

Borders are measured by the yard run and this room with its perimeter of 56 ft. would require 19 yds. Usually the merchant errs on the generous side and no allowance for waste is necessary.

Trimming

The cheapest types of wallpapers are known as pulps, and for various kinds the names are descriptive, such as satinettes, embossed, flocks, high and low reliefs, ingrains, etc. Having obtained the paper, make sure all are of the same shade, and trim off both selvedges. Merchants undertake trimming at a charge of about 3d. per piece, and providing they possess a good machine and an efficient staff, the result is quite satisfactory for ordinary papers.

For better work the craftsman prefers to trim the paper himself. The best results are obtained with a straight-edge and trimming knife. The paper is first cut to the requisite lengths and placed face upwards on the paste-boards, the edge of which is protected by an enclosing zinc strip. The lengths should in turn be dragged forward over the strip, the straight-edge placed accurately over the pattern, leaving the selvedge exposed, and the knife drawn forward firmly and smoothly. The best knives for this purpose have detachable and replaceable blades. Never use a blunt knife.

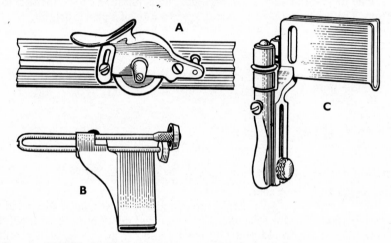

Fig. 3. THREE TYPES OF WALLPAPER TRIMMERS. A. Ridgely.
B. Champion. C. Morgan-Lee.

Special Trimmers

Adjustable trimmers are available. These are set to the required width and pushed along the selvedge, or alternatively the paper drawn steadily through, taking care the guide remains true and tight to the edge. With practice an accurate and clean trim can be obtained. Fig. 3 shows types of trimmers. Best results are obtained by cutting the requisite lengths first and trimming on the boards.

For cheap papers, when an accurate butt is unimportant, the shears may be used. The paperhanger sits on a low chair or stool and with fully extended legs supports the roll by the insteps. The left hand engages the roll as it is cut.

The paper is stretched over his legs to his lap, and he trims with the scissors held in the right hand, rolling up progressively with the left hand.

Cutting and rolling should be separate operations. To roll and trim at the same time causes a wavy edge. The scissors should not be completely closed, so that they may be slid forward enabling the cut to be continuous. Making fresh starts with the shears often results in notches.

Every care should be taken to trim a pattern paper correctly, as too little off the selvedge results in a strip of plain showing between adjoining parts of the motif. Too much removed means an unsatisfactory match, with part of the pattern missing.

Needless to say, equal care should be taken with both edges. Plain papers should be trimmed well in, as the printing may fade a little towards the sides. With cheap work in the past, only one edge was trimmed and the joints lapped. These showed badly on walls with a side light.

WALL PAPERING

Cutting the Lengths

To cut the paper into lengths, first offer up against the wall, unrolling from the skirting to the top. Allow about three inches at the skirting and make a small identifiable mark, a tear will do, about three inches above the top. Lay the paper on the paste-boards and unroll from left to right, allowing the surplus at bottom to trail over the edge of the board. The top mark should show about three inches from the top left hand edge of the table. If patterned, examine to ascertain the best position for cutting.

In the paper illustrated the pattern is such that a whole motif can be preserved without cutting into the pattern above. In this case, if the pattern comes inside the marked length, place a 2 in. wide straight-edge square with its base just touching the pattern. With the right hand grasping the roll, tear sharply across (Fig. 5). This will bring the top of the pattern about $2\frac{1}{2}$ in. below the picture rail if a $\frac{1}{2}$ in. gap is allowed when hanging and subsequently covered with a narrow border. Hanging to a line, cornice or ceiling and subsequent bordering would achieve the same result. With deep borders the gap would have to be widened accordingly. If there is to be no border, the straight-edge should be placed 2 in. higher, to allow an overlap when cutting to rail or ceiling.

More allowance must be made if variations in level are at all pronounced, as often happens in old houses. In this case it is often better to cut half-way through a pattern, a little less in one place and a little more in another would not be obvious, whereas to show a complete pattern in one place and only part in another, would draw attention to the differing levels.

Fig. 4. TWO KINDS OF FOLDING PAPERHANGERS' TABLES.

Having cut the first length, offer it up again to check the length, marking off with about three inches to spare at the bottom when the top is at the correct position.

Match Patterns

With a match pattern such as that illustrated, lay the next section on top so that the bottom, i.e. left hand, is at least as long as the first and adjust so that the pattern matches, making sure that the paper is still long enough at the lower end. Unroll and tear with the straight-edge at the same position as the first. If matching involves the bottom being a trifle short, check again by offering up. Some paperhangers prefer to measure the wall and then the paper, but offering up is quicker and mistakes are less likely.

Fig. 5. TEARING THE PAPER TO LENGTH USING STRAIGHT-EDGE.

Now proceed to cut the remainder of the piece in the same way, storing the short remaining piece under the table. Another 2 rolls can be cut, but more than 3 rolls on the boards become rather unmanageable. Cutting at the same pattern each time ensures simplicity in matching when hanging. It is only necessary to keep the top level at the start, making any small adjustment up or down as required.

63

Drop Patterns

Drop patterns are more complicated as the same level of motif only recurs with alternate lengths (see Fig. 6). This can be ascertained by butting lengths of paper on the table and if the patterns match across in a straight line it is a match pattern, if at a different level—a drop pattern. Cut the second length so that a correct match is obtained, laying it parallel to the first, and exposing about three or four inches of pattern on the further edge. Then the third length can be laid over and matched to the first, the fourth length over and matched to the second and so on. If drop patterns cut to waste, cut from alternate rolls. It follows that if waste is involved with cutting at one pattern, it should be avoided by cutting the alternate roll.

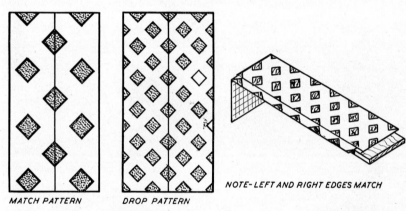

MATCH PATTERN   DROP PATTERN

NOTE—LEFT AND RIGHT EDGES MATCH

Fig. 6. HOW MATCH AND DROP PATTERNS DIFFER.

Paste

Good paste is as essential as good paper. The best is still made by beating 2 lb. of plain wheat flour to a smooth batter and rapidly stirring in a gallon of *boiling* water, forming a thick glutinous mass. A little cold water should be poured over the top to prevent skinning and when the paste is cool it is ready for use after suitable thinning. There should be no lumps, but if present, these must be removed by straining. To obtain good plain wheaten flour today is difficult. Bakers' and household flours contain additives, perhaps desirable for food preparation, but harmful to paste.

Proprietary hot-water paste powders are good and should be prepared similarly, following the maker's directions. Much more handy are the cold water pastes, which are prepared by sprinkling the powder gently into cold water, briskly stirring until the requisite thickness is obtained. Tub paste is ready made and only requires thinning for use. Generally speaking this and hot water pastes are stronger than and possess more slide than cold. There is some doubt as to the suitability of cellulose pastes for papers printed with gold or bronze.

Applying Paste

As a general rule, the thinner the paper the thinner the paste, but this should be adjusted so that it spreads evenly and only freely enough not to drag. Enough should be applied to provide ample slide when folding and hanging. A mistaken notion exists that the hollows of embossed papers should be completely filled with paste. This is wasteful and bad, as only the flush portions

Fig. 7. CONVENIENT ARRANGEMENTS FOR HOLDING DISTEMPER BRUSH ON BUCKET.

STRING TIED ACROSS TOP OF BUCKET

come into contact with the wall. The excess remaining in the hollows may commence to putrefy before completely drying out. A good idea is to tie a piece of string across the top of the pail to support the paste brush, usually a 6 in. or 7 in. flat distemper brush (see Fig. 7).

When the paper is pasted it expands somewhat and ample time for soaking should be allowed prior to hanging. Pulp papers should be pasted two or three at a time, but avoid oversoaking. Heavy papers may require 20 minutes or more. As the paper dries it shrinks and thus eliminates small blisters which may have formed. Excessive soaking however, results in extreme contraction with drying, opening joints and being perhaps powerful enough to fracture the underlying plaster skim.

Assuming that the walls have been properly prepared and sized, all equipment ready, and the cut lengths on the board, we can now commence the pasting and actual hanging. The paper itself should be turned face downwards on the table with the top either to the left or right. The writer prefers the top to the left, but whichever procedure is adopted, it should, from then on, be maintained. The paste pail should be placed under the right end of the table, and the paper laid so that the excess hangs down over the left of the table, drawing the whole forward towards the paperhanger, so that it is about 2 in. over the boards.

The top length is then pushed away so that it just overlaps the further edge of the boards. Paste generously along within a few inches of this further edge, and then brush outwards to the edge. Use the brush in such a way that

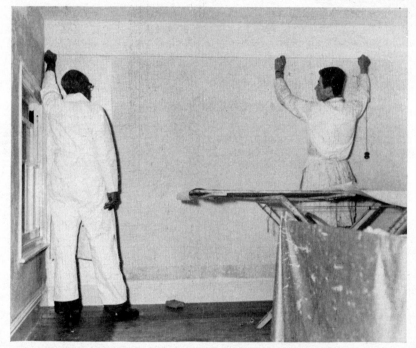

Fig. 8. MARKING LINE ON WALL TO GIVE FRIEZE DEPTH.

it goes off the paper, not towards the edge, thus ensuring that paste does not get under and on to the face of the paper. When completed, move the whole of the lengths away over the further edge, and bring the top, partly pasted length forward so that the edge just overlaps the front edge of the boards or table and complete pasting. Again brush off the edge, with the brush now coming towards the paperhanger. (See Fig. 9).

Folding

When this part of the pasting is completed, lift the ends and fold over just enough to cover the pasted section (see A, Fig. 10), making sure that the fold is square and that the doubled edges run true with each other (see Fig. 11). With the paper still supported by the left hand it can be pushed slightly right or left as required before finally laying flat. Avoid creases and smooth out gently, but do not press or crease the angle down. The dry faces may now be once or twice folded again (see B, Fig. 10) and the whole taken to the right,

Fig. 9. APPLYING PASTE TO PAPER, BRUSH WORKED OFF EDGE.

exposing the remainder ready for pasting, for which the same procedure should be followed.

The completion of the pasting and folding accomplished, the length should be placed on one side over a clean dust sheet, unless cutting is required. Paste the next length and set aside, and so on until the number decided by the quality of the paper and circumstances is completed. A trial with two pasted first should show whether a longer period for soaking should be allowed. Any paste should be cleaned from the hands with a damp wash leather or clean rag.

Hanging

Always commence hanging away from the light, in a normal room working away from the window, right and left. Ascend the steps if necessary with the paper laid over the left arm, face the wall, and, supporting the lower fold of the paper by the instep, gently unfold the top half, holding each edge with the fingers and thumb in front, and place as accurately as possible at the top, allowing the remainder to hang vertically just free of the wall, lightly press the top back, and, if commencing from the window architrave, adjust the edge to this by alternately sliding and lifting if necessary until the edge is

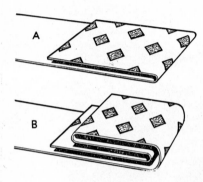

Fig. 10. PAPER FOLDED READY FOR HANGING. The first fold is that of (A), and second of (B).

running true with the woodwork. Fig. 12 shows the early stage of hanging. Check with the plumb line or long level that the paper is upright. If the architrave is out of plumb, the paper will have to be lapped over slightly, plumbed and then trimmed to the edge.

To accomplish this, crease the paper into the angle of moulding and wall, first with the back of the finger nails and then mark down this crease with the point of the shears. Lift away and carefully trim along the marked line. With some papers it may be necessary to use a lead pencil (never an indelible) instead of the shears. Before returning to wall, wipe off any paste from the moulding. Brush out smoothly, working from the centre downwards and outwards as in Fig. 13, lifting by the fold if necessary to remove any creases.

If a border is being hung the paper should be hung with the top edge just below the ceiling or picture rail, allowing at least $\frac{1}{2}$ in. overlap for the border. If there is no border, it should be hung so that there are two or three inches to spare. Against a distempered ceiling or cornice, the paper should now be folded in a narrow strip so that when pressed into position only dry paper touches the distemper. Mark with the scissors or pencil and cut through the doubled paper, removing unwanted portion before returning to wall. Do not cut or mark until sure that the paper is in its proper position. Cut through the line as cleanly as possible, never closing the shears completely, and try to maintain a continuous cut, free from notches. When pressed and brushed back, run the point of the scissors along the junction to enforce tight contact along the edge.

The top half completed, descend the steps and unfold the lower half, holding it free from the wall by the crease as in Fig. 13, brush downwards and outwards. If running out of truth, lift away before attempting to adjust. If the

Fig. 11. FOLDING PAPER AFTER PASTING.

paste is of the right consistency and the wall properly sized, small adjustments may be made by pushing gently to right or left according to the amount of 'slide' in the paste, but every endeavour should be made to let the paper hang itself. If it is running out badly, rehang from the top. If the first length is pushed a little to one side from the middle downwards, the same thing and perhaps more, will be required with every subsequent length. Brush right down to the skirting, and mark and cut with the shears (Fig. 14). Sponge any

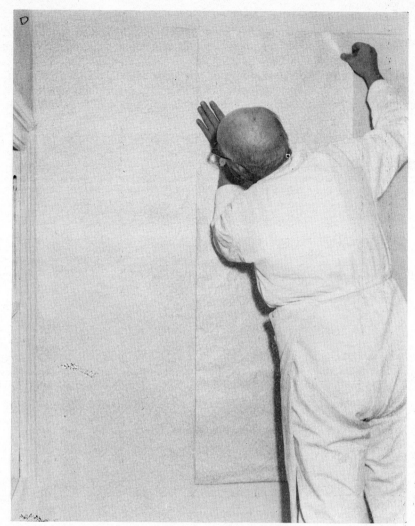

Fig. 12. HANGING PAPER, MAKING JOIN WITH PIECE ALREADY LAID
TO LEFT

paste from the skirting before finally fixing as in Fig. 15, making all tight with
the point of the scissors or back of the finger-nails. Fold the cut-off piece of
paper so that it does not stick to the floor. A plastic pail is an ideal receptacle
for offcuts, as this can be pushed round with the foot without scratching the
floor. The next length can then be hung, following the same sequence, loosely

70

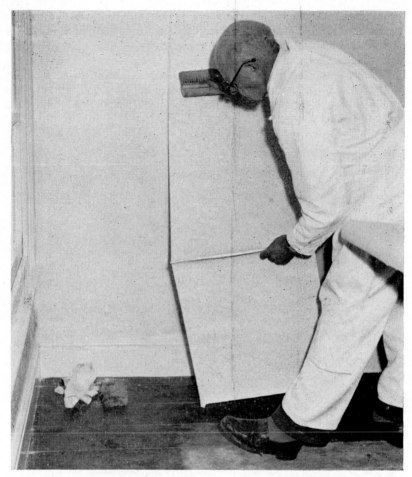

Fig. 13. OPENING OUT FOLD OF PAPER AT BOTTOM.

fixing at the top, and adjusting the match and butt by slight up-or-down and sideway movements until perfect. Checking the match some distance down. The lower folded portion should show whether the butt is running true.

Angles

The next length will probably reach beyond the angle of the room and must be cut before hanging. Never attempt to hang paper round an internal angle, as even a 2-in. strip will crease. Measure from the edge of the last length into

71

the angle and add at least ¼ in. to the greatest measurement, which should be checked at top, middle, and bottom at least. The pasted and accurately folded paper should be placed on the boards, running true with the edge. Marks are made with the shears at the appropriate distance from the meeting edge, and a line drawn connecting these with a straight-edge. Check that the folds are true and the mark is from the hanging edge and cut cleanly through the doubled paper, thus giving a perfectly straight line if the folding is true, but a very wavy one if it is not.

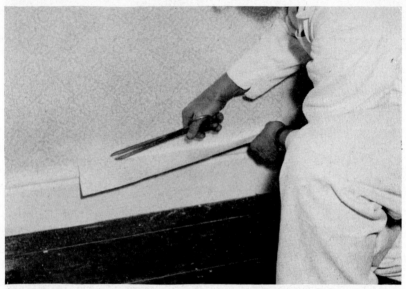

Fig. 14. MARKING PAPER AT SKIRTING FOR CUTTING TO LENGTH.

Hang the first section, pressing into the angle and smoothing down the strip round the return last of all. Then hang the remaining section on the next wall, checking with plumb line or level. This levelling must always be done when changing direction or starting from a fresh point. If the angle is badly out of the vertical (check first) more than ¼ in. lap may have to be allowed, but the greater the lap, the greater the loss of pattern, and consequent distortion.

When approaching the chimney breast the paper should be cut a little bare when hanging the return side, and the length on the front projected about ½ in. beyond the angle. Make sure that all is plumb, and brush the projecting edge round the return to meet or slightly overlap the previous length. With a stiff paper, more than ½ in. will have to be allowed to fold round satisfactorily. In this way the joint will be invisible.

Fig. 15. WIPING PASTE FROM SKIRTING BEFORE PRESSING BACK
PAPER.

The requisite shorter lengths must be cut for above the fireplace. Carrying on when past, hanging the return to the angle before the face length, which should project and fold round as before. Complete to the internal angle, and then round to door. If only a narrow strip is required to reach the architrave, leave for the time being and recommence from the other side of the window and complete round to the other side of the door, where it may quite likely be found that one length will cut into the requisite sections to fill in to the architraves.

If there is a pronounced pattern it may be necessary to fill in over the window, or under, to preserve continuity, hanging the full lengths to match the filling in, and back filling as necessary. With large prominent patterns,

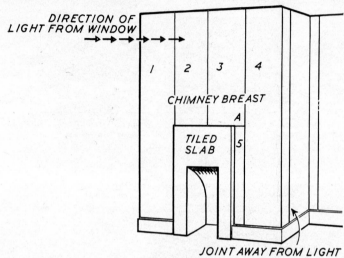

Fig. 16. ORDER OF PROCEDURE AT CHIMNEY BREAST.

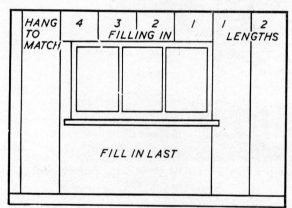

Fig. 17. TREATMENT AT WINDOW WALL.

the chimney breast should be centred by hanging each side of a centre line or with a length in the centre, whichever suits the pattern better. Try to avoid bisecting a pattern on the angles. With contemporary schemes, where the chimney breast is featured with a pronounced design, centring must be observed.

Hanging away from the light can still take place if lines coincident with the widths of paper are first struck. Hanging away from the light ensures that any slight inadvertent overlap will not cause a shadow. When several lengths have been hung, examine the joints and if necessary beat down with the edge of the brush. A boxwood roller may be used over these on suitable papers, but not until the risk of exuding paste is eliminated with lapse of time, usually about half an hour.

Embossed and relief papers cannot be rolled and with many plain ones it is seldom necessary. Beating down with the edge of the brush or the back of the hand is usually sufficient. Avoid excessive rubbing as this may affect the texture of the paper, making it appear darker or lighter at the seams. Always plan the paperhanging to the best advantage before commencing, marking out with charcoal or pencil where the lengths will come.

Windows

When the top of the window is down from the ceiling or picture rail the filling in is done as in Fig. 17. This is essential with patterned papers to preserve the continuity of design. The space beneath the window is filled in later.

If the top of the window is level with picture rail, filling in will have to be done underneath to preserve continuity of design, and the long matching

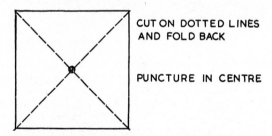

CUT ON DOTTED LINES
AND FOLD BACK

PUNCTURE IN CENTRE

Fig. 18. PAPER CUT TO FIT AROUND SWITCH.

length at the far side hung from this upwards, a rather difficult undertaking. With unobtrusive patterns the filling in can often be done last with a little judicious faking of the pattern at the last seam. Plain papers present no such problems.

When meeting an obstruction such as a switch block, the paper should be cut star shaped or diagonally round it as in Fig. 18. First puncture in centre with point of shears, then make diagonal cuts, when it will be found that the paper can be creased into the edges of the block for marking and cutting. The triangular pieces can easily be lifted away for this. The illustration on page 80 shows this procedure when cutting round an awkward obstruction on a ceiling.

Care of Tools and Apparatus

Utmost cleanliness must be observed, constantly cleaning the hands, tools, and paste-boards. After hanging about a dozen rolls, the paper hangers brush should be washed in warm soapy water, rinsed, and allowed to dry overnight. Congealed paste should be removed regularly from the shears. Pumice stone and water are best for this purpose. Abrasive papers and emery rapidly destroy the cutting edge, which should be treated gently and, when eventually blunt, resharpened by an expert.

Mechanical trimmers occasionally need dismantling and cleaning. Never oil these; french chalk is an efficient and non-clogging lubricant. Wheel and casing knives, Stanley knives, etc., are useful for trimming round awkward obstructions, but care is needed as any unevenness in the underlying plaster and woodwork rapidly blunts the tool and causes notches and tears instead of a neat clean cut. If possible, always use shears (Scissors).

When hanging expensive or heavy ceiling or wall papers, lining should be undertaken first, preferably horizontally or at right angles, with open butted joints.

6 Papering Ceilings

PAPERING CEILINGS PRESENTS slightly different problems, but with the know-how is no more difficult than dealing with the walls, except for the physical strain of supporting the weight overhead. First cut the requisite lengths, allowing about 6 in. spare at each end. The usually longer lengths must be folded concertina fashion as in Fig. 19. When hanging, keep the top uppermost and it will be found that the paper unfolds automatically as one proceeds (See Fig. 20). Support the pasted and folded paper by an odd roll of paper which holds it flat across the ceiling as shown. Commence by pressing the first unfolded section into position, supporting the remainder by the roll just under the ceiling. Slide and adjust until running true, then make the next unfolding, support again, brush carefully, making sure of butt, and so on until the further side is reached.

If all is satisfactory, mark and cut off to the cornice, or, if there is no cornice, cut with about an inch to spare to run down the wall, thus making sure of there being no gap at the junction when the frieze or wall is subsequently dealt with. Figs. 21 and 22 show the stages in the work. When hanging successive lengths make sure of a butt joint and of course matching if pattern is present.

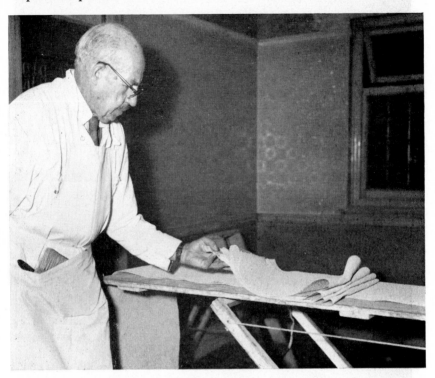

Fig. 19. PAPER FOLDED AFTER PASTING READY FOR LIFTING.

Obstructions

Reference to the Figs. 23 and 24 show how awkward obstructions may be dealt with. The ceiling illustrated was being papered with a pebble dash duplex paper, very heavy when pasted, and tending to separate into two layers if oversoaked. Incidentally, the hanging would normally be planned so that the electric light fitting is at the edge of a length rather than in the middle. This could have easily been achieved by cutting in half the first length and papering the frieze first, but the more complicated way was chosen as a demonstration. The work was undertaken on a dark November afternoon, otherwise the light fitting could have been temporarily removed.

Fig. 20. FIRST STAGE IN PAPERING A CEILING.

Fig. 21. CONTINUATION OF ABOVE. NOTE ROLL SUPPORTING FOLDS
OF PAPER.

Lining Papers

Lining papers are, of course, the simplest to hang and, if possible, lining should be practised before attempting heavier papers. As soon as sufficient confidence has been attained, paste two at a time, sufficiently soaking to ensure that any small blisters shrink out on drying. Make sure that all joints adhere, and leave a gap of about $\frac{1}{32}$ in. at the butts. This will fill in with the subsequent distempering. The slight gap is much easier to maintain than a dead butt, as any overlap will show, whereas the gap will prove invisible. Always hang away from the light to minimize cast shadows caused by inadvertent laps.

Lining papers are 22 ins. wide and classified by weight. No. 480, a good general purpose lining, weighs 480 lb. to the ream. For weak plaster, or over hardboard with butted joints and for similar use, a reinforced lining is avaliable. This is practically untearable. As a preparation for papering over matchboard and similar surfaces liable to opening at joints, hessian skrym is first affixed with strong size and copper tacks.

Fig. 22. THE LENGTH NEARING COMPLETION, CREASES BEING BRUSHED OUT.

79

Fig. 23. CUTTING CEILING PAPER AROUND ELECTRIC LIGHT FITTING.

Fig. 24. HOW PAPER IS CUT AROUND CEILING ROSE.

Heavy Papers

Heavy relief papers require considerable soaking, it being sometimes advisable to damp all the paper first with clean cold water. This not only stretches the material, but also makes it much more pliable. Special adhesives must be used. Dextrine is one of the best and is mixed by soaking the powder, a glucose, in water overnight. Rubber glue is more tenacious, but sets too rapidly except for small borders, for which it is essential when applying over Lincrusta or painted surfaces. Anaglypta is a hollow relief, Lincrusta is rather like linoleum with a smooth back.

Coved Cornices

A coved cornice is supplied in Anaglypta in flat 12 yd. rolls. First the ceiling and walls are struck with charcoal lines about 4 in. from and parallel to the angle. Drawing pins are partly inserted in to the ceiling line at two foot intervals, and the soaked and dextrine-pasted strip pushed up with the edge

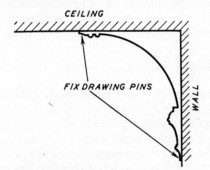

Fig. 25. SECTION THROUGH COVED
CORNICE IN ANAGLYPTA.

under the pins. When the line is met, the drawing pins are pressed home. The cove is formed by running a roll of lining paper along horizontally until the bottom edge is level with the wall line and temporarily fixed with drawing pins pushed in just under the edge. Only sufficient of the edge should be pasted to ensure adhesion. There is no point in wasting adhesive in the hollow part.

The first strip should run the entire length of the wall, and the internal mitres subsequently scribed. External mitres are butted and templets are supplied for both. When dry, remove the drawing pins and apply at least one coat of oil paint before any distemper or plastic emulsion. The oil paint will prevent the absorption of any atmospheric moisture which would probably distort the cove. Relief papers should also receive this treatment, and where condensation occurs, all papers should be protected with an impervious coating, such as varnish or clear plastic emulsion.

Borders are usually printed in strips right through the roll. For ordinary work, paste right across, fold accurately, and carefully cut out along the selvedges. Imperfect folding results in either under- or overcutting on the reverse. Make sure that the folds are true and maintained true while cutting. For better work, the borders should be cut with knife and straight-edge prior to pasting.

Many varied schemes can be undertaken with wallpaper, from classical to the so-called contemporary idea of using contrasting papers in the same room. This and other aspects will be discussed in a later chapter dealing with design in general. A successful scheme depends on the correct relationships of paper, paint, and distemper considered as a whole in their environment. Paperhanging is so varied a craft that it merits a whole volume, but the writer has endeavoured to cover some of the salient points within this rather long, but we hope not wearisome chapter. Many techniques exist, some work from right to left, others prefer the reverse. The keen student should practice on the lines suggested using the basic principles to establish his own interpretation of a craft which in some ways almost approaches the status of art.

Papering Difficult Surfaces

Painted walls, especially high gloss, present special difficulties as condensation may cause staining, loss of adhesion and shrinkage at joints when subsequently drying out. The painted surface should be washed with sugar soap and rubbed down to remove all traces of gloss, rinsed, and leathered off. The surface should then be sized. A handful of plaster added to a pail of size and continually stirred during use will present a slightly gritty film, which when rubbed down with dry glasspaper, will tend to hold the paper in place. The walls or ceiling should then be cross lined in the opposite direction to the final papering. Over walls subject to severe condensation or rendered impervious by the application of damp-proof solutions, a special sheeting known as Kotina may be applied. This is a cellular plastic which imprisons so much air that it is always warm to the touch. Five sheets will cover the same area as a roll of paper and it is fixed by applying a special adhesive to the plaster, the mterial being trimmed into position with a sharp knife. This should be lined before papering.

In any case cross lining should always precede the hanging of expensive or heavy papers and when there is any doubt as to the suitability of the surface to receive paper. Vigorous brushing, and, if necessary, repasting can be carried out on lining paper to secure adhesion, when it is obvious that such treatment would spoil a delicate paper.

7 Craft Techniques: Graining

THIS MOST ANCIENT craft, graining, has suffered an eclipse, though there is some evidence of its revival. Aesthetically, the slavish imitation of expensive woods in an endeavour to make common deal appear as if it were oak, mahogany, or walnut, cannot be justified, but the representation of the colour and texture of beautiful woods as an integral part of a decorative scheme may be one of the best ways of achieving a harmonious general effect. Providing that the graining is a frank interpretation of the decorative qualities of the timber and not an attempted fake, it would seem difficult for the most determined purist to object.

The aim should be to interpret the fine timber in terms of paint, symbolizing rather than imitating. No other method can provide such rich deep luminosity of hue and texture of fine wood short of its actual use either in the solid or in veneer. No brown paint approaches the glowing hues of well-kept and polished furniture. These hues and tones depend on the richness of natural colour in the wood itself, possibly enhanced by judicious staining and polishing. Graining achieves this by superimposing transparent staining pigments over an opaque ground. It depends entirely on its handling to provide at once the richest effects of dark timbers to the subtle transparencies of light woods such as maple and sycamore.

The technique may best be explained by the time-honoured practice of graining in oak. Indeed it has been said that once this has been mastered, all other woods are simple. Probably the first grainer was inspired by the woody appearance achieved when trying to make a dark brown paint cover over a cream. The first operation is, of course, to prepare the surface up to undercoating stage as perfectly as possible. Contrary to common belief, graining accentuates rather than obscures defects.

Ground Coat

The final coat before the actual graining is known as the buff, and should be of the same hue as the lightest part of the wood to be imitated, or perhaps a shade paler. At least a day should be allowed for drying, in cold weather longer.

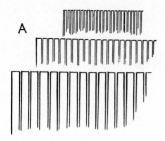

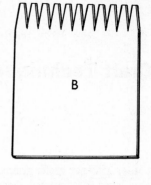

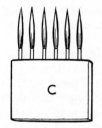

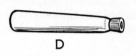

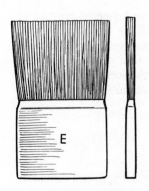

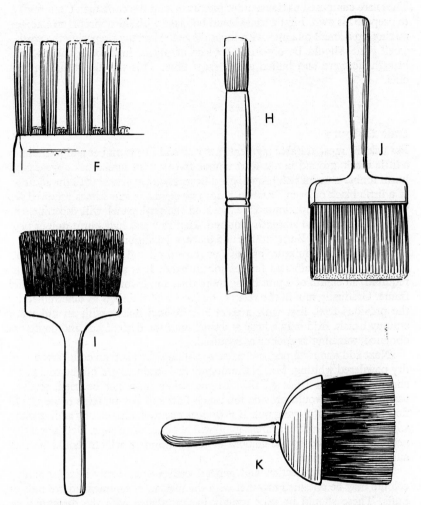

Fig. 1. TYPES OF BRUSHES USED BY THE GRAINER. A. Steel combs in sets and grades, 1 in., 2 in., 3 in., and 4 in. wide. B. Leather comb. C. Pencil overgrainer. D. Eye dotter for maple. E. Thin hog hair overgrainer. F. Overgrainer with parts of hair cut away. G. How thin hog hair overgrainer is used. H. Hog hair fitch. I. Badger softener. J. Hog hair softener. K. Dusting brush.

Scumble or Graining Colours

These are composed of transparent pigments, and the craftsman often prefers to prepare his own. First a trial should be made with the appropriate stainers, mixing up a small quantity with turps. When originally preparing the work a small panel should be obtained, a piece of ply or hardboard will do, and brought forward and buffed at the same time. This will be useful for try-outs.

Oak Colours

For oak the most suitable pigments are raw and burnt umber and sometimes a little black, ground in oil. Raw umber gives a cold fumed oak appearance, burnt umber a warm rich brown. Modifications are achieved with the addition of a little black or even Prussian blue; raw sienna is sometimes required for very light effects. Sparing applications on the trial panel will ascertain the type of pigment and strength required. Half raw and half burnt umber provide a medium oak. Burnt umber and black, a Jacobean effect, and so on.

Next put out a mixture of half raw linseed oil and half turps into a paint kettle, using just sufficient for the job in hand. It is surprising how little is required, an eighth of a pint being more than ample for the average door and frame. Gradually mix in the relative quantities of stainings as determined by the previous trial, first with a palette knife and finally with an old worn stumpy brush. Add only a little at a time until the desired hue and depth are obtained, warming or cooling as required.

Next add about $7\frac{1}{2}$ per cent paste or patent driers and an equal amount of dry powdered whiting. Mix in thoroughly and strain. Clean off the trial panel and make further trials on this. Liquid driers must not be used, as their varnish content would provide too much flow and any patterns made would flow out instead of staying put. If flow does occur, counteract by adding more whiting. This being transparent in oil will not alter the colour. Depth or lightness may be varied by the amount of added thinners which should be half and half oil and turps.

For ease of application and general convenience ready-mixed graining colours may be obtained together with the makers' recommended grounds or buffs. These should be used strictly in accordance with the directions, as some must be thinned with turps only. Slight modifications may be achieved by intermixing or the addition of fine stainers. An excellent substitute for the patent driers and whiting is clear glaze. This is a special wax medium which, when added to the graining colour, ensures that the grain produced by combing, etc., retains its pattern. Add just sufficient to the mix to ensure this; usually about 10 per cent. is the maximum. Too much would have a harming effect.

Application of Scumble

For application partly worn brushes should be used, and the colour spread evenly and rather sparingly over the surface. If an ordinary four-panel door is being done, brush in the two top panels, matching the depth of each. Cross and lay off until the wash is perfectly even before attempting any actual graining. Wipe off with rag any colour deposited on the rails and stiles. Then with a graining brush, often known as a 'drag' or a duster, Fig. 2, commence to form the grain by laying the drag at a slight angle to the work at the bottom of the panel, and, with a slightly nervous rocking motion, draw it upwards for about two inches, separating the scumble into woody streaks as in Fig. 3.

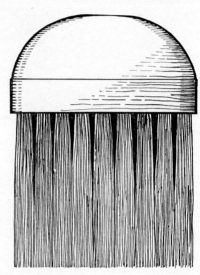

Fig. 2. DRAG OR DUSTER USED IN THE EARLY STAGES OF GRAINING.

Complete all the bottom and then commence at the top. Lay the brush right into the top joint, give it a steady shake or two, and then carry on with a slight nervous rocking and waving motion right through to the bottom. The reason for the preliminary graining at the bottom now becomes apparent, as the inclination of the drag or duster prevents it reaching to the extremity.

The greater the pressure, the more pronounced the grain, and vice-versa. Thinner and more liberal applications also produce more open grain, but are difficult to control and also tend to flow out owing to excess medium. Experiment on the spare panel with differing pressures and wavy motions with different mixes, to find the technique best suited to the work in hand, always endeavouring to maintain a clean and even appearance. Have a sample of the real wood if possible, and try to interpret the character of the plain grain as nearly as possible.

Fig. 3. USE OF DRAG TO FORM PRELIMINARY GRAIN MARKING.

Fig. 4. COARSER MARKINGS PUT IN WITH COMB.

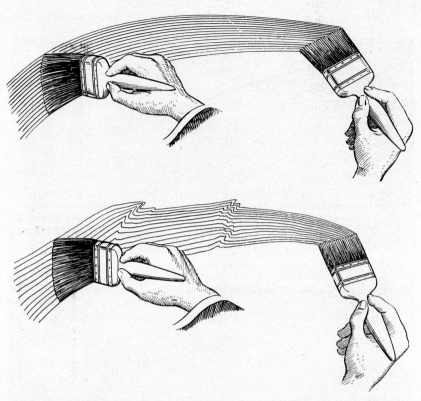

Fig. 5. VARIED MARKING PRODUCED BY MOVEMENT OF BRUSH.

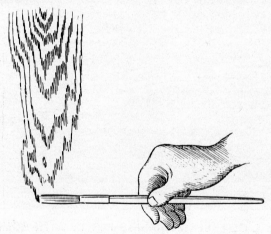

Fig. 6. PAINTING HEART OF OAK FIGURE WITH VEINING FITCH.

Coarser or more open effects are obtained with the use of steel and rubber combs of varying or graduated fine and coarse teeth, Fig. 4. The comb should be dragged with a similar rocking motion, straight through the work, wiping clean. More natural effects are obtained by again combing obliquely to the first, perhaps with a different grade comb, thus breaking the lines into more realistic forms. Experiment will reveal the possibilities of infinite variations, such as using a wide comb at one side of the panel, a medium in the middle and a fine to complete, merging from one to the other, or, alternatively, using a graduated rubber comb. Crossing rhythmically with a wavy motion produces markings suggestive of medullary rays and may be used as a basis for further wiping out. The alternately straight and oblique use of a coarse graduated rubber comb, broken with transverse steel combing can suggest the plainer effects of heartwood.

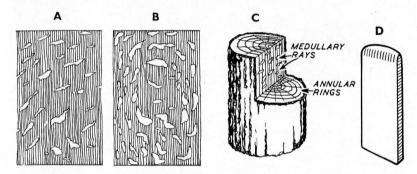

Fig. 7. DETAIL OF OAK GRAIN AND FIGURE. A and B. The fleck marking of figured oak. C. Log cut away showing figure (medullary rays) produced in quarter-cut wood. D. Graining horn used to wipe out figure.

Figured Oak

When, and only when, the plainer parts of the wood can be successfully represented, the process of figuring may be attempted. First, however, a few words on the formation of grain patterns. The medullary rays, figure, or silver grain are composed of starch and sugar cells which radiate from the heart outwards, and, being less absorbent than the remainder of the wood, resist absorption of stain and appear lighter in consequence. As the rays radiate from the heart outwards they are best displayed by radial or quarter sawing, forming what used to be known as wainscot oak.

Fig. 7 shows a split log and reveals how the annular growth rings become the alternate dark and light streaks in the vertical section. The rays nearest the heart are thin and only slightly inclined to the direction of the grain, becoming broader and more oblique until about half-way, when they assume pronounced and decorative forms almost at right angles, gradually merging into less definite forms as the outer part of the tree and the sap wood are approached.

The vertical streaks are fine at the heart, formed in the early days of growth, becoming progressively coarser outwards. The figuring also shows the evolution from youth to maturity, the outer and less definite having not had time to completely develop. Generally the figuring is of an elongated S shape, tapering at the extremities, and radiating rhythmically from definite loci. No figures should ever cross or appear about to cross each other.

Examination of an actual piece of quartered oak will show how the rays subtly twist and turn to line up with the adjoining rays above and below and slightly to the side. Note the variation in size and form and observe that even

Fig. 8. GRAINING HORN IN USE.
The position of the rag on the horn is constantly changed.

violent changes of direction evolve from ray to ray. The pattern depends as much, or perhaps more, on the spaces between the rays as the often fantastic forms of the figures themselves.

Examination of the real wood shows the infinite variety of form and spacing and at the same time a homogeneity which links the design into a harmonious whole. Do not use ply or veneers as samples, these are often cut in such a way that the figure is repetitive and grossly distorted.

Forming the Figure

The actual representation is achieved by a process of wiping out. A piece of horn, thin bone, or plastic, shaped like an elongated thumb, is enclosed in absorbent non-linting rag in such a way that the rag can be constantly pulled over the graining horn, so that clean rag is always available as wiping out proceeds. About three or four wipes can be made before changing slightly. The horn is held in both hands as in Fig. 8 and the figure wiped out progressively, commencing at the top, planning the design as one proceeds.

Holding the horn parallel to the direction required produces thin markings, and the width is increased by changing to an oblique angle, achieving the greatest width when at right angles. A nervous, rhythmic motion, continually varying the angle will produce lifelike figures. The real beauty is only achieved by constant practice which eventually results in controlled accidental forms approximating to the infinite variety of nature. Every endeavour should be made to create a rhythmic radiating and varied pattern, seeking inspiration from the real wood.

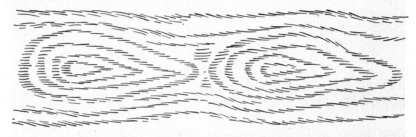

Fig. 9. HEART OF OAK FIGURING.

Further examination of the latter will reveal fainter markings between the main figuring, and these may be represented by forming a pad of rag, folded about four times to the requisite width and lightly dabbed and dragged off where required. The width depends on the dimensions of the fold and the depth by the amount of drag, which must be quite gentle. By holding the rag in both hands between forefingers and thumbs it may be bent to shapes conforming with the surrounding figures. If the work appears a little harsh it may be lightly softened by gently drawing a softener or dry drag over the whole, being careful not to muddy or obscure the figuring. Unwanted figures may be subdued by dabbing lightly with the folded rag, making them resemble the other faint background markings. If in any doubt, leave well alone, as afterthoughts are seldom an improvement on original ideas, and alterations always show.

Heartwood

It has become an established tradition to represent the heartwood on the lock rail of a door, Fig. 9. Two methods are available, both effective when well

Fig. 10. WIPING OUT OAK FIGURE AFTER GRAIN HAS BEEN COMBED.
Both hands should be used. One hand is withdrawn here for clarity.

Fig. 11. TAKING OUT HIGHLIGHTS WITH RAG PAD. The figure of natural oak should be followed.

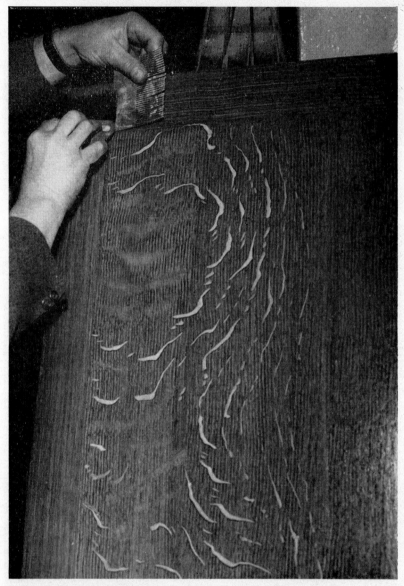

Fig. 12. METHOD OF STRIKING A CLEAN JOINT.

executed and appalling when not. When wiping out, the veining horn may be used for the finer markings, but for the broader work the tip of the thumb enclosed with rag is best. The same process of wiping out should be used, but each oval form, working from the inmost, must be completed with each enclosing ring accentuating features of the inner ones.

Avoid regular ring-like shapes and do not place exactly in the centre. Try to introduce the variety displayed by an actual sample and at the same time relate the design to the shape of the rail itself. Do not make the letter plate the obvious centre of a design. The outer work is completed by using a coarse to fine graduated comb, following the general direction and structure of the heart grain, but gradually straightening towards the outside edges.

A steel comb is then lightly dragged right through, slightly obliquely and with a little wave here and there to break up the hard edges. Finally a light combing radiating at about 40 degrees from the centres adds verisimilitude and variety. Incidentally, the lock rail should not be grained until the rest of the door is completed. A wide comb held vertically over the joint with the stile will prevent encroachment. The muntins are treated in the same way.

Alternatively and more realistically, though less decoratively, the heart grain may be represented by brushing in in the normal way and then removing part of the colour by lightly rubbing a rag through the width to be occupied by the pattern, and softening right through with the drag to give an even gradation from the darker outer edges to the centre of the lighter strip. Allow a little time to set after combing the outer and darker strips. Then with a thin flat fitch or writer's pencil paint in the dark forms, using slightly stiffer colour rather sparingly and break up the hard lines by judicious and varied combing.

The outer combing should be planned to harmonize. Instead of the brush application the grain may be drawn in with an oil bound or wax crayon, sharpened to a chisel edge. With this the outline should be lightly sketched in and then completed with short broken dashes to simulate the actual open grain. The comb would not break up solid lines.

Joints

We may now return to the actual door which we started so long ago. When the panels are complete, with their mouldings carefully brushed in with care at the mitres, the usual sequence of muntins, rails and stiles must be observed. The joints must be struck cleanly and this is best achieved by masking the completed member with a steel comb held across the joint, so that the back is perfectly in line. This is shown in Fig 12.

The whole of the framing should be brushed in evenly, maintaining an even tone, before any work with the drag or comb is attempted. If the panels are figured, keep the surrounding work reasonably plain as a contrast and foil. Very fine effects of close grain may be obtained by 'flogging', i.e. hitting

H.D.—G

lightly and obliquely with the flat edge of the drag or duster. The duster or a hog hair softener is best for this, the handle giving balancing leverage. Relief work, carving, etc., is often best dealt with by stippling. When all is dry it must be completed by varnishing, but time and cost permitting, it may be greatly enhanced by overgraining.

Overgraining

Traditionally overgraining was always undertaken with water colour, a process still unrivalled for subtle gradations of depth, luminosity and richness. As an oil painted surface resists the even application of water colour, it must first be prepared by sponging over with a paste composed of fine whiting and water until all evidence of cissing ceases. Sponged and leathered off the work should now be ready to receive the water colour glaze. If cissing still occurs, more treatment with whiting is necessary.

Water colour is traditionally made from Vandyke brown ground in water and perhaps a little ivory black. A little stale beer is added as a binder. Nothing better has been devised, though some grainers use Fuller's earth for the purpose. The beer provides just enough adhesion to resist the pull of the varnish brush, but should be used sparingly as any excess might crack the varnish. About one part of beer to twenty of water should suffice. A thin wash should be spread over the work and divided into varying bands of colour parallel to the grain by means of a hog hair overgrainer.

Overgrainers are available as separate pencils mounted in a tin ferrule, or the bristles of a plain overgrainer may be separated by the teeth of a comb. The darker veins thus formed greatly enhance the depth and colour, but the overgraining must be carried out with the utmost restraint to avoid too great a depth and streakiness. Finally soften and allow to dry. Never attempt more than two panels at a time as the water colour dries so rapidly that control soon becomes impossible. A great deal of judgement is required, as the colour dries out many shades lighter and only the varnishing restores its true depth. Without experience, one may easily find the final result much too heavy.

Beautiful effects may be obtained over heart grain by spreading a thin, even wash over the whole and removing radiating fan shapes from the centres with a small piece of wash leather, finally softening. A badger hair softener is best for use in water colour. Never spoil it in oil paint.

Characteristic of oak is the multiplicity of fine short dark lines, due to the absorption of filler and stain by the open grain. These may be imitated by flicking on colour with a flogger and breaking up with cross combing.

Fig. 13. OAK GRAINING. FIRST STAGE IN WIPING OUT HEART WOOD.

Fig. 14. OAK GRAINING. BREAKING UP HEART GRAIN WITH COMB.

Special Roller

The effect is readily achieved by using a roller, made up of a number of serrated, freely revolving discs. A brush charged with the overgraining colour is mounted with a clip to the handle and the whole pushed, not drawn, over the work, which must be prepared by flatting with whiting as for brush over-graining. The feeding brush may be detached and recharged as required.

A special end grain roller is made to fill to the ends of recessed panels, etc. These dark lines or checks are absent from the medullary rays and must be removed from these with the damp wash leather. The whole process of overgraining may be carried out with ready-mixed scumbles or graining colours in oil if preferred, but never quite so effectively as with water colour. Oil paint should be removed from brushes thoroughly after use, preferably with one of the modern brush cleansers.

The whole process of oak graining can be carried out in water colour, but unless complete control of the medium is attained, oil techniques are much simpler. Water colour lends itself to the exploitation of accidental and charming effects, but with oil paint almost unlimited control is possible. The artist uses water colour for its evanescent beauty, oil paint when he requires complete mastery of his subject.

Modern Ideas

Today, the time honoured veining horn and rag is being superseded to some extent with the use of rubber or cork. A wedge-shaped typewriter eraser wipes out with extreme facility, and its flexibility lends itself to the rapid creation of interesting and beautifully varied figuring. After every two or three wipes, clean the edge with rag held in the palm of the hand. Chisel edged and slightly rounded edged pieces of cork can similarly be used. However, both these methods lack the subtlety of the veining horn in practised hands, and wipe out so cleanly that strong contrasts between graining colour and ground must be avoided. Softer effects are obtained by enclosing the rubber with rag. Also the rubber tends to leave a thin dark line under each figure, attractive but unnatural.

Dark Figure

Under certain conditions of weathering or chemical treatment, the medullary rays sometimes appear darker than the ground. To achieve this effect, the figuring is painted in with a thin flat fitch or pencil when the preliminary brushing in, dragging or combing has partially set. A slightly thicker colour must be applied sparingly to avoid runs.

Much modern furniture is finished in a light shade, sometimes preserving the colour of the wood as the plane leaves it. This is imitated by preparing a light, almost broken white ground. The tendency of yellowness in really light scumbles may be countered by adding a little flat white, used sparingly; too much leads to a muddy, cloudy appearance.

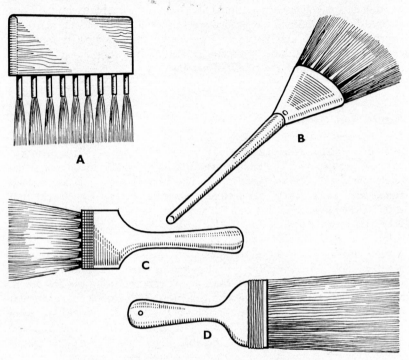

Fig. 15. BRUSHES USED IN GRAINING. A and B. Overgrainers.
C. Softener. D. Hog hair flogger.

Limed Oak

Limed oak is easily simulated by working on a buff ground, just a shade more intense than the darkest part of the work to be imitated. The graining colour should be prepared by mixing clear glazing medium with flat white or off-white, and brushed, dragged, and combed in the usual way, the darker figures being subsequently wiped out. An attractive and quick way is to use the roller overgrainer charged with the white alone, subsequently wiping out. Needless to say the varnishing of light effects must be undertaken with a really pale varnish. An eggshell finish looks most natural with this and over all oak finishes.

Root of Oak and Pollard Oak

These are usually grained in rather dark warm tones. Both have extremely twisted, curly grain, pollard having swirls of grain surrounding small knots, from which radiate writhing figures. Knotted oak is similar but without such pronounced swirls and with larger isolated knots. The knots are formed by twisting on stiff colour with a stumpy fitch or even by dabbing with the paint-covered finger-tip. Small star-shaped cracks may be wiped radially across the larger knots, which may also have a thin light rim wiped partly round the circumference. All of these are greatly enhanced with overgraining in which a mottled effect is added to the general striping.

Maple and Sycamore

The representation of light woods such as maple or sycamore may be undertaken in a similar way to that used for light oak, although, of course, no medullary rays are present. The grain varies from fairly widely spaced wavy lines to elongated and delicate heart forms. The more subtle effects are best obtained with water colour, but, before attempting successive coats, the individual washes must be sealed with a coat of thin gold size or varnish and turps. When this sealing coat is dry, flatting with whiting will again be necessary before attempting further washes.

The bird's eye, so decorative a feature of maple, may be imitated by the use of a maple dotter. A cheap way of preparing one of these is to use an old round writer. Cut the bristle off short and square, burn out the centre with red-hot wire to form just a ring of stiff bristles. This is dabbed on to colour spread on a palette, then dabbed on the work in little groups, the size being varied with the pressure and aided with twisting movements. The wing shapes may be spread out with the tip of the little finger; indeed the finger may be used for the whole operation. Fig. 16 shows a bird's eye maple panel.

Previously to the dabbing the ground should be glazed with a wash of scumble or water colour, then mottled, either by use of the mottling brush (very much like a plain overgrainer but thinner and softer, often camel hair), or by merely beating with a crumpled piece of soft paper and softening. The mottler should be used with a rocking and lifting technique, the tips of the bristles being as capable of lifting as applying colour.

The mottles should be in rhythmic, slightly curved parallel bands, crossing the main direction of the grain. The paper dabbing gives a more broken mottle, suitable under bird's eye effects. The transverse mottles are best suited to plain grain and sycamore.

The thin wavy lines are drawn in lastly with a writer and the enclosing denser lines with a pencil overgrainer following the general direction. Plain maple and sycamore are treated in this way, sketching in the heart grain first angles produces varying spacings. Used completely edgeways only one line would be produced, and all possible variations from the narrowest to the widest can readily be produced. Sycamore is generally much more delicate than maple and the underlying mottle should be correspondingly restrained. Always refer to the real wood, never copy other people's graining as this can only result in an imitation of an imitation.

Fig. 16. PANEL IN BIRD'S EYE MAPLE.

Mahogany

Mahogany may be simply imitated by working on a ground produced from venetian red and orange chrome, using vandyke brown as the graining colour. Much better effects are obtained, however, by working on an ochre buff and applying a wash of burnt sienna which should be first mottled and then somewhat vigorously flogged. This gives the effect of the underlying flecked

103

Fig. 17. MAHOGANY. DRAWING GRAIN WITH DRAG.

appearance and a rich luminous ground on which to carry out the feathery grain so characteristic of Spanish mahogany. Figs. 17 and 19 show a mahogany panel.

This is best carried out in water colour, using the pencil overgrainer at varying angles to produce the beautiful elliptical forms. Final strengthening of the patterns and swirls may be drawn in with the writer with deft touches, some continuous, and others just here and there as design and fancy dictate.

So-called mahoganies such as sapele and gaboon are comparatively easy to represent. The former has slightly wavy parallel stripes which may be laid in by using the brush sideways, the tips applying and the sides of the bristles removing simultaneously. Softening should be lightly carried out at right angles to the grain. This gives realistic effects of broken waviness present in

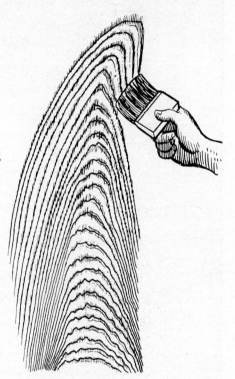

Fig. 18. GRAINING MAHOGANY. Note the system of converging lines.

most hardwoods. This softening must not be heavy enough to form transverse streaks and should just be sufficient to drag out the sometimes too definite streaks.

Spanish feathered mahogany has a pattern similar to the Prince of Wales Feathers and appropriately enough, a tail feather from a game bird or cockerel is an excellent tool to draw this pattern with. Width of stroke can be varied at will, using just the tip or even the entire length. A sort of pencil overgrainer can be formed by removing parts of the feather. Fig. 22 shows the stages in the work. 'Fiddle Back' is a mahogany rich in elaborate, deeply contrasting mottles.

Fig. 19. MAHOGANY. CROSS SOFTENING USING SOFTENER.

Walnut

Walnut grounds are usually cool buffs, and the graining colour raw umber with judicious additions of burnt umber and sienna in the warmer, and ultramarine blue and ivory black in the cooler and greyer tones. Mottling should be rather pronounced though well softened. Too restrained, it would not

Fig. 20. MOTTLING
GROUND FOR
WALNUT.

Fig. 21. MANIPULA-
TION OF SOFTENER
OR DUSTER FOR
MOTTLING WHEN
OVERGRAINING.

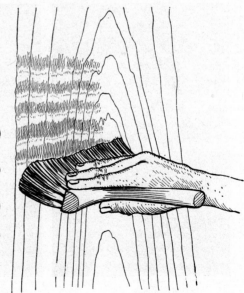

Fig. 22. CURL MAHOGANY. Three stages in graining this highly intricate and attractive hardwood.

Fig. 23. WALNUT MATCHED VENEERS, SHOWING USED OF DRAG.

Fig. 24. WALNUT. USE OF BRUSH TO DRAW GRAIN PATTERN.

show through subsequent elaborations of grain such as displayed by good veneers of Italian walnut. The writhing, involved, and streaky grain can well be drawn in with the feather, pencil, or overgrainer, the plainer enclosing work being completed with the latter or even the drag. Softening at right angles provides the right measure of indefiniteness, and a deft touch here and there will re-define and provide accents where necessary.

Fig. 25. PIGEON'S WING USE TO DRAW WALNUT GRAIN.

The best results are achieved by several separate processes; flecking, mottling, main grain, and accentuating, and a final wash of varied warm and cool glazes. When carrying out such a complicated process, remember that each successive wash will darken the work.

Keep the work on the light side. The final glaze will provide all the depth and richness required. It is impossible to lighten grained work, but darkening is easily achieved.

111

Built-up Patterns

Matched veneers can be imitated by scoring lines co-incident with the veneer joints, using a fine, sharp knife and a straight-edge, just penetrating the buff. When the scumble is rubbed in it remains in the grooves giving a guiding line for the division of the grained patterns, and appearing similar to the actual joint in the veneer itself. Fig. 23 shows a matched walnut panel being grained, and Fig 24 a later stage showing cross-banding.

The grain must match in reverse in each section. With sufficient confidence this may be done with an overgrainer in each hand, forming the pattern with the right hand and allowing the left hand to repeat each movement in harmony. Anyone who practised scales on the piano in contrary motion knows that the left hand will accurately mirror the movements of the right.

This scoring with the knife technique can prove extremely useful when dealing with large flat areas such as flush doors. Scoring two lines down a flush door will suggest three separate boards, each of which can be grained as a separate entity, not matching but keeping each in character. When graining matchboard, endeavour to introduce variety and yet maintain balance. Avoid even repetition such as one plain, one figured, and so on, occasionally giving adjoining two figures, and now and then showing heartwood or coarse broken combing.

Always realize the actual structure of the timber. A square oak post could not have strong medullary rays on adjacent sides, the flat top would be concentric arcs, formed by the annual rings. Similarly only the finest medullary rays approach anywhere near the heart grain.

Graining is an essentially personal craft, and in the days of the master craftsmen everyone knew who had grained a front door. His style was as individual as his signature. Painters going by would say, 'Look old Jim has made a fine job of that so and so door.' Always have a sketch book handy to note and record exciting examples of grain structure. The pleasure in first seeing and then interpreting will be twofold.

8 Marbling

As WITH GRAINING the representation of marbles is largely a lost art, but occasionally the decorator has to attempt this ancient craft. Although not a marble, polished granite is often employed as one, and its representation is readily achieved. For grey granite a medium grey ground is prepared, and first white and then black spots are spattered evenly over the surface with a special graniting brush or a rubber stippler, as regular a distribution and tone as possible being maintained. For pink granite use a pink and white spatter on a grey ground or grey, white and black on a dull pink ground. In any case the ground colour should match one of the middle tones or hues of the actual stone.

Light Marbles

These require a white or off-white ground, preferably semi-gloss. When this is completely dry it is oiled out by rubbing over with a rag dipped in half-and-half linseed oil and turps and wiped nearly dry. This assists the softening of the preliminary stages of glazing and mottling, hard edges tending to melt away. Siena marble is generally creamy in tone, gradating to deep patches of warm buff and golden tints. Over the ground, spread a wash composed of white with varying quantities of raw and burnt sienna, mixing the pigments in a medium of turps and a little gold size or varnish.

Pools of colour on the palette should be modified by adding pigment as required, and the varied tones spread over the work, mottled and blended, using the softener continuously to maintain the soft translucent melting tones of the actual marble. A nearly dry turpsy rag should be used to wipe out high lights.

Exquisite mottlings may be obtained with flicks of a feather, especially if this is laid on the palette to pick up varying tints along its length and then applied with a gentle irregular swirling motion. When dry the veining should be carried out. The colours of the veins vary from warm to deep cool almost violet greys, best mixed from varying proportions of white, black, cobalt blue,

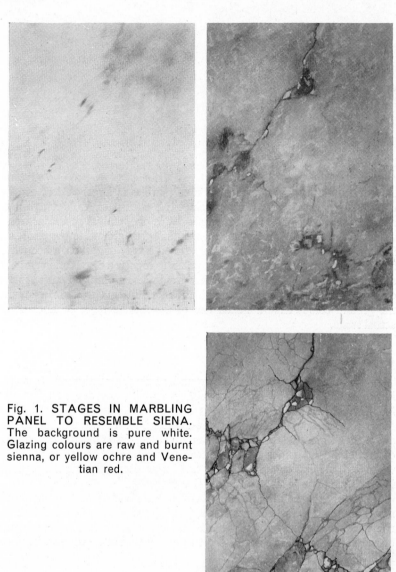

Fig. 1. STAGES IN MARBLING
PANEL TO RESEMBLE SIENA.
The background is pure white.
Glazing colours are raw and burnt
sienna, or yellow ochre and Vene-
tian red.

and light red. The veins may be drawn in with a writer or feather and softened as the work progresses, subduing as if partly under the surface in places and emphasizing where the vein comes right to the surface. Again, as with graining, carefully study real samples and note the subtle variations of direction, colour, and depth.

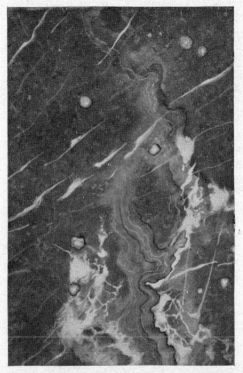

Fig. 2. RED DEVON MARBLE. Background is soft, mauvish red with variegated slate-grey patches over which are groups of strong white veining.

Carrara Marble

Statuary or Carrara marble is represented on a light grey ground, glazed with a translucent wash of pearly white, partly wiped out in uneven irregularly placed patches of grey, still partly osbcured by the white. Careful wiping out will suggest veins just under and coming to the surface. Darker veins may be drawn in with the feather or brush. Thin translucent washes of a light colour over a darker ground give the peculiar cold milky appearance of marble, which in thin enough flakes is itself translucent.

115

Bréche Marbles etc.

Bréche rose and Bréche violette, also alabaster (not strictly a marble, really a crystalline gypsum) are also imitated on a white ground, rose with soft pink and violette with soft varying violet mottlings. These marbles have suffered

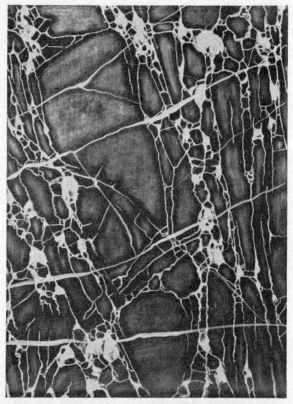

Fig 3. BLACK AND GOLD MARBLE. Background is black. Graining colours are Oxford ochre, white, and burnt sienna.

fracture and under pressure and heat have become re-cemented and present an appearance of something like a mosaic of differently coloured and shaped pebbles.

Apply a fairly intense and varied mottle, and spatter here and there with spots of turps. These spots will rapidly spread, exposing a partly creamy ground eventually surrounded with a thin dark line of pigment, much more delicate than could be obtained with a brush. The shapes will be irregularly oval or circular, and may be enlarged or modified by further spatters. When dry delicate veining with greys and violet will complete.

Alabaster is creamy and translucent deepening in places to a rich deep old gold with subtle purple patches. Purple brownish veins occur spasmodically and whitish veins sometimes appear over the darker parts.

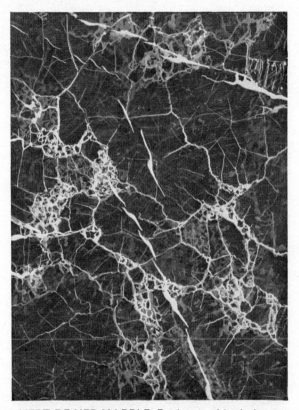

Fig. 4. VERT DE MER MARBLE. Background is dark green with grain markings of green and filmy white.

Veining seldom follows the basic structure of the marble, often crossing fossils and pebble-like forms at acute angles. When the marble was first formed, millions of years ago it was subjected to intense pressure and heat, causing fracture and cracks. Deposits of various coloured minerals, sometimes thousands of feet thick, eventually covered the marble-forming limestone and eventual percolation of rain water filled and cemented the cracks with the

117

various coloured mineral solutions. Green from copper, violet from manganese, yellow and red from iron, and so on. An appreciation of its evolution should help in its representation. So many and so varied things have gone into making the marble, that the forms appear accidental, and its representation is best achieved by carefully controlled accidental handling of the glazes and washes.

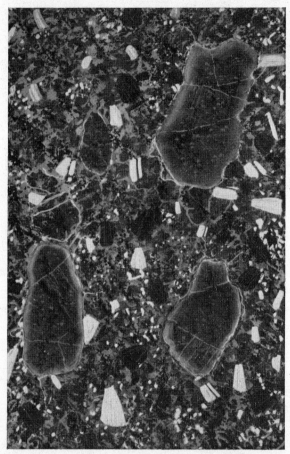

Fig. 5. VERT ANTIQUE MARBLE. Ground colour is black or dark greenish black with markings of varying tones of green and black and grey patches.

Dark Marbles

Dark marbles are best worked over a black, grey, deep brown, or green ground, the thin lighter scumbles readily creating the translucence. Black and gold is veined with a varying golden colour prepared from orange and lemon chrome, white and ochre, over a black ground with patches of soft translucent grey in isolated patches between knots of encircling veins. An occasional whitish vein may also be present, crossing the golden ones at an acute angle. Black Belgian marble sometimes has a slightly greyish cast with long irregularly parallel streaks and veins.

Verte antique or verde antico should have a black or very deep green ground, over which should be spattered a medium grey green with lighter greens progressively over the top. Wipe out roughly oval and circular dark blotches here and there, and finally vein lightly with thin light green and white. Well thinned veining gives an illusion that the vein is just below the surface, thicker and more opaque veins appear on the surface. Vary the strength of veining as it proceeds.

Porphyry, rouge royal and similar require a black or dark purply brown ground, stippling first with a brownish red spatter. A venetian red mixed with a little white is superimposed in a coarse stipple, and roughly ovoid fossil shapes with broken white, varied in tone are painted in. Finally it is veined with translucent to more opaque white. A few brownish and dark veins may be introduced over the lighter parts.

Cedar Onyx

This is a brown marble with a swirling striped grain, similar to a coarse grained timber, but with much wider streaks in places. It may be represented with a graining technique with uneven spacing of the flowing lines. Swedish Green may be similarly treated, working on a pale grey green mottled and varied ground, and streaking with varying shades of grey, grey green, and black. Gently softening across the veins and strengthening here and there, wiping out an occasional fossil or pebble shape should complete these and similarly striped marbles.

The craft of marbling can well be exploited in the treatment of bath panels and the like, and its use provides a decorative and durable treatment for dadoes in busy corridors and staircases. Many Italian buildings have expensive marbles in the entrance hall and first flight of stairs and excellent painted marbling on the remainder, often so well done that it rivals the real article in appearance. All marbling should be protected with varnish, using very pale crystal varnish for the lighter effects.

Whole text books have been written on the subject of graining and marbling and the student would do well to refer to these (if still available) in the local library. This one chapter has of necessity been limited to a very brief description of basic principles.

9 Plastic Decorating

DURING THE days of wallpaper famine just after the war, a great deal of plastic decoration was undertaken to relieve the monotony of bare distempered walls, and its use is still popular for certain purposes. The acoustics of a building may be markedly improved by the application of relief textured surfaces, as these break up and diffuse echo effects, hence their use in many cinemas. A serious objection is that heavy reliefs provide dust traps in their indentations and their ultimate removal is a messy and expensive operation. For their application a non-absorbent sound ground, preferably broken white flat oil paint, is required. The material is usually in the form of a powder which should be gradually and thoroughly mixed into water to the consistency of a very thick cream, allowing ample time for the powder to absorb all the water possible. Any dry powdery lumps would obviously not adhere.

Application

The mix is applied to the surface with a filling knife or stiff brush to an even thickness, dependent on the amount of relief required. Deep relief requires an exceedingly stiff mix, lower reliefs, thinner mixes. Manipulation with various tools provides diverse effects. Antique plaster effects are obtained by swirling the brush or knife in overlapping spirals, pebble-dash by the use of various grades of rubber stipplers, this being one of the easiest ways of achieving an even texture.

Beating and lifting with a flat board produces interesting twig and small tree-like forms. Coarse combs present interesting textures which may be curved, commencing so that each pattern edge is cancelled by the next. By combing horizontal and vertical squares alternately to the width of the comb, interesting basket patterns are produced. When the material is dry, excessive relief and sharp points should be removed with glasspaper mounted on a block, dusted down, and primed and painted in a plain ground colour according to the final decoration required, or just left plain. The paint should be 'long oil' to satisfy porosity. Over the prepared ground a glaze of suitably thinned pigments will enhance the appearance tremendously. Fig. 1 gives a variety of effects.

For an antique plaster effect spread a transparent glaze composed of glazing medium, turps, raw sienna, and a little umber and white on a white ground. Stipple with a hair stippler, beating hard to open the glaze and when partially set, go over the whole with a rubber squeegee or a piece of rag stretched over a broad knife. This will remove the glaze from the high spots and give the effect of the patina acquired with age.

OBLIQUE COMBING   SHELL PATTERN   BASKET WEAVE

BRUSH PATTERN   ROUGH CAST   TREE FORMS

Fig. 1. VARIOUS PATTERNS SUITABLE FOR PLASTIC DECORATING.

Sun-rise Effects

Variation of the pigments can provide interesting broken colour effects, and mottles of harmonizing and even contrasting colours give opportunities for endless variety. Alternatively the glaze may be graded and a suggested sun-rise effect may be achieved as follows, working on a white or off-white ground.

121

Fig. 2. STIPPLING PLASTIC COATING WITH CRUMPLED PAPER. This
gives the effect of Morocco leather.

First prepare sufficient glazing medium to cover the whole work, and divide equally into two kettles. To the first add sufficient lemon chrome and a little white to obtain the lightest shade. To the second add sufficient deep orange chrome to form the darkest shade. In between these kettles place three more and into the centre one pour half the light and half the dark. From the centre kettle to the outside ones again pour half-and-half, making five evenly gradated tones in all.

Mark lightly the surface into five equal spaces by striking faint lines and paint in the top division with the lightest colour. Follow with the next using the second kettle, and so on, completing the bottom with the deepest colour. Skilful use of the brush aids in blending one strip with the next and is finished by stippling with a hair stippler from light to dark, being careful not to go back on the work once the stippler has picked up darker tints. Highlights may be removed with a squeegee if required.

Particularly charming effects may be obtained by using this technique over tree patterning, the white twigs, after wiping off, suggesting a coating of hoar frost against the rising sun. Other hues can be used effectively, but must progress in chromatic order, for example, blue—blue green—green—green yellow—yellow and so on. Never attempt to blend complementary colours as only muddiness will result in the intervening shades. Graduated effects can be much more readily achieved by spraying technique, but on limited areas, skilful blending and stippling achieves perfectly good results.

Smooth Surfaces

Similar effects of glazing may be obtained on smooth surfaces, the technique of application being the same, but with infinite possibilities of patterning. Hair stippling provides a fine oatmeal effect, rubber stippling coarser in proportion to the grade of stippler, resembling shreds of tobacco if a brown glaze is used. All the work should be hair stippled first to obtain a completely even tone and texture.

Beating with crumpled lining paper as in Fig. 2 gives a morocco leather effect, rolling upwards with a rag or wash leather an interesting broken effect, rather softer than the former. Experiment will reveal endless possibilities. Wiping the glaze from the raised portions of mouldings and carvings helps to create pattern and relieve monotony. With old carved work the retention of deeper colour in the hollows accentuates age.

Broken colour effects may also be achieved with distemper and plastic emulsion paints, but the speed of drying makes control somewhat difficult. To obtain translucency distemper should be thinned with half-and-half water and petrifying liquid, using clear plastic medium instead with emulsion paints.

10 Stencilling and Sign Writing

STENCILLING IS A craft worthy of revival. As a rapid means of repeating a decorative motif in borders it is only equalled by applied wallpaper borders, and these may not always harmonize with the particular scheme, whereas design and colour in stencils may be varied at will. The design is prepared, and is then drawn to size on stout cartridge paper or pasteboard, taking care that a section of the repeat is included.

Making the Stencil

Inherent in the design are the necessary ties, which if carefully planned, not only strengthen and hold the stencil together, but enhance the design. For example ties at the joints of stems and leaves in floral motives provide accent and emphasis to the structure and form. Ties must always be present in enclosed forms to prevent the centre falling out.

The unwanted portion is cut away with a stencil knife or sharp penknife with the paper placed over a sheet of glass. When cutting is complete both sides of the paper should receive two coats of shellac knotting to stiffen and strengthen it. This also assists in cleaning off deposited paint.

Using the Stencil

Stencilling colour should be fairly stiff and placed on a palette. Having struck the necessary guide lines, the stencil plate is placed accurately in position and secured with stencil pins (rather like slender, small stilettos) or drawing pins. The colour is picked up from the palette with a stencil brush, which is rather like a cut-off shaving brush, but with extra stiff brustles, and pushed through the incisions in the stencil plate with a dabbing technique, the body of the stencil preventing any colour except that of the design reaching the surface. The process is shown at (C), Fig. 1.

The inherent stippled effect is one of the charms of stencilling and should be maintained as evenly as possible. Colour thin enough to flow out evenly would run under the edges of the stencil and a semi-dry technique should be

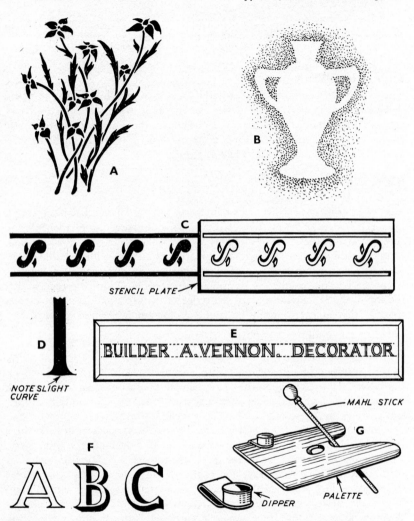

Fig. 1. DETAILS OF STENCILS AND APPLIANCES USED, ETC.
A. Typical leafwork stencil.   B. Edge stencil.   C. Repeat pattern and its
stencil.   D. Serif of Roman lettering.   E. Example of lettering.   F. Shadow
lettering.   G. Tools of the sign writer.

observed. When the first section has been completed, remove the stencil, wipe
clean and refix so that the necessary key to the repeat overlaps and repeat
until the whole border is completed. Two or more colours may be used, by
designing separate stencils for each colour and ensuring that they register

125

accurately over each other. Each colour must be dry before further application. Stencils may be sprayed, but adequate masking must be undertaken.

Edge Stencilling

This is a modern technique particularly adapted to spraying. It is used round the outer edge of the cut-out design, fading away from this into the background. Fig. 1 shows the idea at (B). Similar, though not quite so subtle effects can be obtained by using a stencil brush, gradually reducing the amount deposited outwards and hair stippling.

SIGN WRITING

Sign writing is a specialist craft which can only be mastered with constant practice. Thorough knowledge of the forms and characters of the different scripts and alphabets is essential plus an instinctive feeling for good spacing. Mathematical divisions, though helpful, are only an approximate guide. If the same space is left between each varying letter an appearance of extreme irregularity would result. For example, the letters W O can be placed so that the top of the W nearly overlaps the bulge of the O; A and V can be closely spaced, whereas E I D would be cramped with similarly close spacing.

Roman Lettering

Roman lettering does in some measure lend itself to geometric arrangement, the letters themselves conforming to regular proportions. O is circular, E half as wide as high, and so on. The height of I may be eight times its width; F four times; and C would be like O, as wide as it is high.

On these lines the word Office might be spaced with letters 8 inches high as follows: 8 in. for O, 1 in. for space, 4 in. for F, 2 in. for space, 4 in. for F, 2 in. for space, 1 in. for I, 2 in. for space, 8 in. for C, 1 in. for space, and 4 in. for E, thus requiring a rectangle 8 in. high by 37 in. long.

Many systems such as this have been devised, but the practised signwriter just strikes his top and bottom lines and lightly sketches in chalk a skeleton of each letter. Working to a carefully outlined drawing is never attempted as it prevents the free manipulation of the brush. If the brush is allowed to run freely over the work without the restriction of guiding lines, it will form far more confident and decided strokes. Slight deviations from geometrical accuracy are part of the charm of good lettering.

Serifs

Probably the most popular alphabet in use today is Trajan Roman, based on

ABCDEFGHIJKL

MNOPQRSTUV

WXYZ1234567

890

ABCDEFGHIJK

LMNOPQRSTU

VWXYZ12345

67890

Fig. 2. EXAMPLES OF ROMAN AND SANS SERIF LETTERING.

inscriptions on the Trajan Column in Rome. Its somewhat rigid form is a result of the limitations imposed by the exigencies of carving in stone. Probably the serif was introduced as a preliminary cut across the direction of the main stroke to minimize the risk of the stone splitting too far under the chisel. Be that as it may the serif assists the writer in making a termination to his stroke and is a decorative addition assisting legibility.

For some reason the eye seems to tire when reading 'sans serif' (sans is French for without). Nevertheless, lettering based on GILL SANS SERIF is almost as popular as Roman and suitable for contemporary work. Earlier in this century sign writing was of a much freer and flowing type, often florid and flamboyant, giving full reign to the dexterity of the writer's pencil.

An Example

To proceed to the actual lettering, we have taken as an example a typical fascia. Having decided on the size and type of letter, guide lines are struck level at the top and bottom limits (see dotted lines, E, Fig. 1). A fine line of sufficient length is rubbed with chalk or charcoal, stretched taut from marks at each end, pulled away by means of a centre loop (tied first) and allowed to snap back, leaving an imprint. Any excess should be lightly flicked away, not rubbed. The lettering is lightly sketched in, with careful checking of the spacing to make sure that it is symmetrical.

The colour is next prepared, tried for consistency and opacity, and a little put into a dipper, which is a small tin with a clip soldered underneath to allow fixing on edge of palette. A similar dipper should contain medium or turps. The palette is held by the thumb hole, the hand grasping a mahl stick underneath. The latter is a piece of cane or dowel about 30 in. long, with a circular pad of wadding enclosed with wash leather tied to the end, so that it may rest without damage on the work and steady the hand (G), Fig. 1. The pad should rest to one side and either over or beneath the letter, whichever is more convenient. On this the hand holding the brush can be comfortably rested and steadied while making the stroke, the mahl stick being moved constantly as required.

Writing the Letters

A writer should be selected just wide enough to extend to the full width of the narrowest part of the lettering. This may be too large for the beginner, who often prefers to use the round-pointed pencil, but the best results can only be obtained with the long, flexible flat chisel-like writer. Long strokes are made with this by laying the brush with almost all the hairs touching the work. The underpart wets the surface progressively ahead of the tip, assisting slide and definition while resisting lateral wavy movement. With a third of the hair on the work any tendency to hand shake is also largely restrained, but the use of the tip alone means that involuntary movement in any direction may occur. The chisel-edged tip is used solely for fine lines such as serifs.

Spread a little colour on the palette, pick a little up by drawing the brush through the pool of colour, laying the bristle or hair flat and parallel. Commence to form the serif at the top of the letter, using the tip longways, i.e. at right angles to the main body of the letter, come round the curve by gentle pressure and then straight on down the left-hand side of the letter, curving round into the bottom serif, and completing the bottom of this with a slight serpentine line (see D, Fig. 1). Repeat down the other side of the letter, making sure that the sides are parallel, in the right direction, and of correct width.

The brush under guidance does more than half the work, and the best shapes are always obtained by exploiting the inherent capabilities of the brush. Pressure widens the stroke and vice versa. Occasionally the writer may have to be rinsed in the medium to keep clean. After use it should be washed in warm detergent, rinsed, and greased with tallow, the hairs being carefully laid out to their proper shape. The tallow will, of course, have to be thoroughly removed with turps before further use.

Colours

The colours themselves must be of the finest quality and those contained in tubes are economical and clean in use. Often two coats are necessary. The first should be sharp, thinned with turps alone. For finishing work colours are thinned with special medium or raw and boiled linseed oil, with a little varnish added to increase gloss, and turps to increase flow.

Perspective Lettering

Elaborations of lettering are obtained by outlining with contrasting colour, or obtaining relief by depicting simple cast shadows. Alternatively letters are still more convincingly shown by painting a modified perspective representation of a cubical form, enhanced by darker tones on the undersides, and with blended shadows on the curves where they would logically appear, the whole reinforced with a cast black shadow. Leaving a small space between the letter and its return edge and shadow is very effective and provides an additional outline. Outlines may also be separated from the letter.

Various Alphabets

A few years ago a fashion sprung up for so-called contemporary lettering, at its best a bizarre distortion of classical form, sometimes emphatic, but often an illegible and hideous caricature. The test of good lettering is legibility,

H.D.—I

suitability for purpose, and skilful execution. Italics are used for emphasis and variety. The inclination must be rigidly maintained. Small or lower case letters are used when space is restricted, and the alphabet should conform with the capitals or upper case.

Script somewhat resembles copper plate handwriting, but do not attempt a slavish imitation, rather preserve the characteristic brush forms. Gothic or Old English, various mediaeval and ecclesiastical styles may be used when appropriate, but most of these lack legibility. Some beginners have difficulty in deciding which strokes should be thick or thin, if in doubt, write the letter with an ordinary pen, the upstroke will be thin and the down thick when writing naturally. The Roman alphabet contained no U; V was used in its place, but the slavish following of the antique can lead to such ridiculous signs as BVTCHER or PLVMBER. A letter U was devised which obeyed the canons of Roman design, as were also the series of Arabic numerals, unknown to Rome.

11 Gilding, Lining, Murals, etc.

FOR THE BEST sign writing, gilding is employed. Gold leaf is prepared by beating the extremely malleable metal to a film so thin as to be translucent, and light enough to be readily airborne, so avoid draughts as far as possible when using it. It is usually purchased in books of twenty-five leaves about 3 in. square, interleaved with thin tissue paper and known as English transfer gold leaf, the best being 22 carat.

Application of Gold Leaf

When gilding lettering on a sign board, the surface is first pounced with fine whiting enclosed in a muslin bag, the fine powder thus being evenly spread over the whole surface. Lines are struck, letters sketched in, and written over with gold size to which a little chrome is added sometimes. When this is tacky a leaf of gold is pressed with its paper backing uppermost on to the sizing. The paper is lifted away, and any remaining gold pressed over other sized parts as required, until all the gold has been transferred as economically as possible.

Rubbing the back of the transfer paper with the finger tip, or, better, with a piece of wadding assists its transference. Make sure that there are no holes. A slight overlap does not matter as this will eventually brush off. Japan gold size dries rapidly and can be gilded shortly after application; oil gold size remains tacky for about 24 hours.

When gilding is complete and dry the surplus is easily removed with a pad of cotton wool, it being found that the gold cannot adhere to the pounced whiting, which is then sponged off and leathered dry. In place of whiting a preparation called glair is used for the best work. This is a wash prepared from weak isinglass and fine whiting or french chalk, brushed over the whole surface and allowed to dry. After gilding, it is fairly easily washed off.

Gilding on Glass

Plate glass fascias present special problems, working in reverse being involved. First prepare an exact drawing of the lettering on stout lining paper, trace it through to reverse, and mount it in position on the face of the glass which must be perfectly clean and dry, especially on the reverse side to be gilded. The size used is isinglass or gelatine. If the letters are to be outlined or shaded, this should be done first and allowed to dry. The water size should be flooded on but not so generously that it runs, and gilding follows fairly quickly.

To carry this out the loose gold leaf is placed a sheet at a time on the felt-covered base of the gilders tray which is shaped like a 6 in. box with top and one side missing. It has a leather strap beneath to take the thumb (see A, Fig. 1). To lift the leaf, a thin flat brush known as a gilder's tip is used (B). This is drawn through the hair first, and absorbs enough natural grease to enable it to readily pick up the leaf from the book (not transfer for this purpose) and transfer it to the tray, where it is gently laid flat on the felt, a light puff of breath assisting. A stronger blow would cause the gold to float away.

It may be found easier to make the transfer by picking up the gold with the gilder's knife which has a very thin oval blade as at (C), Fig. 1. With the knife cut a strip of gold just wider than the letter, pick it up with the edge of the tip and lay it gently over the sized work. It will be found that when the gold leaf approaches within about a quarter of an inch it miraculously flies of its own accord flat on to the surface, far flatter than if the gilder attempted to smooth it on with wadding.

Allow a slight overlap when completing, and when all is dry clean off with cotton-wool. Examine carefully for any misses or pinholes, and if any, re-coat with size and touch up with odd scraps of leaf. Economical cutting is essential with such an expensive material, but do not skimp so that touching in is necessary at the edges and laps.

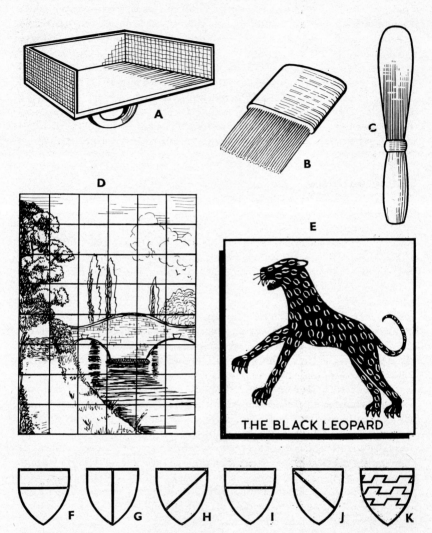

Fig. 1. DETAILS OF GILDING, LINING, MURALS, ETC. A. Gilder's cushion. B. Gilder's tip. C. Knife used by gilders. D. Pictorial sign or mural. E. Conventional rendering of an animal. F-K. Shields used in heraldry.

Backing

The work now has to be backed up with paint, again reversing procedure, though, of course, any shading or the like should be completed. It is best to undertake all this before gilding. The mirror-like quality of the glass makes the use of a gloss paint unnecessary, but the first coat is paradoxically the finishing in colour and texture. A grained or marbled effect requires the graining before the buffing; stippled grounds must have the stipple applied first, and so on. With marble the veining must be done before the mottle. For a plain paint finish the first coat must be of the correct hue, thinned with turps and bound with Japan gold size. The next is a normal undercoat, and the finishing coat an elastic gloss paint.

Gilded lettering on glass doors is often left unbacked. In this case a sealing coat of varnish must be applied, overlapping the letters by about $\frac{1}{8}$ in. or more for larger letters. Without this protective coat, condensation, let alone washing, would rapidly attack the edges which would progressively become more and more ragged. Over the lettering itself may be applied a backing coat of black or other desired shade after the varnishing. Outlined letters, even if outlined first as they should be, must receive this backing treatment with varnish.

Gold leaf is permanent on a properly prepared ground. After writing a fascia or sign in gold leaf the background should be varnished. This requires great care as the varnish must be cut up to, but not touch the gilding. Varnish over gold gives a brassy effect and tarnishes increasingly with age. Silver and aluminium leaf are treated in the same way. Silver only on the back of glass, as if exposed to the atmosphere it quickly tarnishes.

Aluminium is used for face work, though tending to dull with exposure. Both are much thicker than gold, so lapping must be kept to a minimum. A cheap imitation gold leaf is made from Dutch metal. This rapidly tarnishes unless varnished and should only be used inside. Metallic or bronze paints may be obtained in all shades, but are much more suitable for painting radiators and ironwork, though permissible for temporary signs.

Lining

The sign writer is often called to execute lining. The boundaries of the lines are first measured and struck with the chalk line. Long lines require two men to hold the string across the guide marks. The lining may be carried out with sign writer's brushes, preferably a liner, and filled in with a larger brush. Lining is carried out by painters, using a lining fitch along a straight-edge with the bevel held inside. The bevelled lining fitch should be drawn edge-ways along the straight-edge, which should be placed the thickness of the brush below and parallel to the guide line. The lining fitch should be slid along the straight-edge just up to the line, continued along the top, care being taken to wipe the straight-edge clean after every stroke. Take special care that no runs occur when cutting in the lower edge. Fill in with a conveniently sized flat brush. For narrow lines, a thin fitch which will not spread wider than the required width must be used, and an endeavour made to complete with one stroke.

Murals

The decorator and sign writer is often called upon to execute pictorial signs and simple murals. A scale drawing should first be prepared and painted up to the required finish. Assuming that the prepared cartoon is scaled one inch to one foot, lines should be drawn horizontally and vertically at one inch intervals, forming a series of squares across the drawing as at (D), Fig. 1. For extra accuracy diagonals may be drawn across squares containing complicated detail. With the sign or wall correspondingly squared at one foot intervals, the drawing may be accurately and easily transferred. Numbering the squares may be of assistance. Enlarging often means that small work requiring artists brushes can be readily reproduced with ordinary paint brushes.

Pictorial sign work should be bold and simple, and murals conceived in terms of flat areas of paint, rather than fussy detail. Good drawing is essential and simple colour harmonies should be maintained. For example, the mural in Fig. 1 was painted in autumnal tints to harmonize with the warm creams, browns, and buffs of the walls and woodwork, and was carried out by second year students of Reading Technical College under the supervision of the author. It could equally well have been conceived in the delicate yellows and greens of spring, the full colour of high summer or the silvery greys of frosty winter, to harmonize with any appropriate general colour scheme.

Inn signs give wonderful scope for the decorative artist, and many fine examples of this art may be seen all over the country. With those with heraldic motives, care must be taken to ensure that the details conform with the rules of heraldic design. In representing animals such as lions the claws and teeth are always exaggerated to give a fearsome appearance (E), Fig. 1.

Heraldry

The heraldic painting of shield and emblems occasionally comes within the decorator's province. One of the many excellent text books on this subject should be referred to when carrying out this work, to ensure correct delineation. Its origins go back to the days of chivalry, and the terms used are Norman French. Argent means silver or white, sable—black; or—gold or yellow, and so on. The colours are represented in black and white by arbitrary hatchings. Vertical divisions of shield are known as per pale, horizontal—per fess, diagonals as bars.

12 Staining, Varnishing, and Polishing

STAINING TIMBER MAY be simple or complicated, and may vary from the treatment of floors to the imitation of marquetry. Before staining, make sure that the timber is clean and dry. Any paint spots must be eliminated with a paint remover, though it is better to take precautions to avoid them, because they completely resist absorption of the stain. With floors, etc., any projecting brads should be punched home, and for good work stopped with hard stopping tinted to the hue of the finished stain. If plain stopping were used, this would resist penetration and appear as light blobs. Mixing pigments into stopping softens it, but this may be remedied by the addition of a little dry, powdered whiting, until tackiness vanishes but plasticity remains. Face up the holes before staining. Any glasspapering should be in the direction of the grain.

Types of Stain

Many proprietary wood stains are on the market, and, if using them, follow the makers' directions implicitly. Except for the cheapest work, so called varnish stains are not to be recommended. The right technique is to stain and varnish in separate operations. A cheap and reliable oak stain may be prepared by thinning decorators' black japan with turps, the strength depending on the amount of thinners. Make trials first on an odd piece of similar timber. Burnt umber added to black japan gives a rich brown oak colour, and the addition of burnt sienna gives a rich mahogany shade. These can be varied in hue and tone by adjusting the relative amounts of stainings and turps.

Staining should proceed regularly, making sure of wet edges and brushing out evenly. The dilution should be such that the stain readily penetrates, but do not overthin. Best results and the clearest revelation of grain results from rubbing over with rag after brushing. This lifts excess from the less absorbent grain, accentuating the natural beauty of the wood and ensuring evenness of general tone. Soft absorbent woods however, may perhaps be best left just with the brush, as with these low-grade timbers unpleasant darks may occur in the regions of knots and sap wood.

Softwoods

When staining old floors, make sure that all old wax polish has been removed, as any residue would prevent penetration and drying. Bare places should be touched up to match the remainder and allowed to dry before general staining. Where it is desired on new work to get an even finish over softwood of varying porosity, a weak coat of glue size should first be applied, just strong enough to equalize without entirely preventing suction. Unfortunately this will result in a loss of definition in the grain, and trial should be made to assess results of absence or presence of size. To preserve the natural colour of the wood it is essential to size before varnishing, unless one of the modern clear finishes is used.

Manipulation with graining tools in the wet stain by dragging, flogging, and combing may help to make a common pine or spruce to resemble a more expensive wood. A roller with a series of sharply serrated steel discs will imitate the check markings in oak, and filling these indentations with thick dark pigment and rubbing the excess from the surface with rag, may at first glance deceive even the expert. However, these methods savour of undesirable faking, but, as the customer is always right, it may be necessary to submerge one's own taste to satisfy another's vulgarity. For temporary display work such faking can be effective and perhaps justified.

Hardwoods

Hardwoods present few difficulties, as absorption is usually even though somewhat slight, and staining is only necessary to accentuate hue and tone. Some woods such as teak contain natural oils which resist penetration and tend to prevent drying of oil stains and varnishes. In these cases use proprietary stains and make trials first. Water stains are used more as a preliminary to french polishing than for varnishing, but over clean wood are effective. They are obtainable as crystals which are dissolved in hot water and used cool. Water staining raises the grain of the wood and this must be smoothed with fine glasspaper, always working in the direction of the grain and never crossing over the joints of rails and stiles. For varnish it is economical to size over the stain, but two coats of varnish are much more durable.

Varnish

For the best work the first coat of varnish should be undertaken with body varnish, and two or three days allowed for drying. This is then sponged over and rubbed with a flat pad of felt dipped in pumice powder until the shine disappears and all is smooth. After rinsing and leathering dry the finishing coat of varnish is applied.

Varnishing painted work is an operation seldom carried out today, though no gloss paint or enamel possesses the brilliance and depth obtained by varnishing over properly prepared flat colours. These flat colours should be ground in turps and bound with gold size. They used to be known as coach colours.

Varnishes are made by cooking natural or synthetic resins and gums in linseed oil thinned with turps. A long oil varnish contains much oil and is very elastic; in 'short oil' varnish the turps predominates, and is harder and more brilliant. Outside varnishes are usually the former; short oil varnishes are suitable only for inside work, where hardness is more important than elasticity. General purpose varnishes are claimed to be equally suitable for exterior and interior work, but the use of a material especially prepared for a specific purpose is usually more satisfactory.

Application of Varnish

Best work should receive a minimum of two coats of varnish, and should be felted down between coats as previously described. The varnish should be applied with a full, even coat, crossing and laying off as with paint, but without vigorous brushing which would cause frothing. The latter would result in pinholes or a sandy appearance when dry.

Never undertake varnishing in damp or cold conditions, or when condensation is likely to occur before the material is dry. These conditions cause blooming, a flat opaque misty film, much akin to the bloom on grapes. Frost will leave an indelible imprint on all gloss finishes. Always endeavour to varnish in warm, dust-free conditions. When working outside, first thoroughly sweep pavements, etc., and, as an added precaution, lightly sprinkle the paving with water occasionally to prevent rising dust.

To avoid contaminating the varnish with particles inadvertently picked up with the brush it is a good idea to have the varnish in a small kettle placed inside a larger one, using the outer one for scraping excess over the edge when necessary and only dipping the clean brush into the inner kettle. After use varnish brushes should be rinsed out in white spirit and suspended with the bristles immersed in raw linseed oil. If placed in water, blooming would ensue when next they were used in varnish.

Flat Varnish

A popular finish over graining is eggshell flat. This is obtained by superimposing a coat of the flat varnish over a preliminary coat of glossy body varnish, which should be first felted down with pumice. It is just possible to omit this and work direct over the gloss, in theory a sound practice, but in fact exceedingly difficult. The flat varnish initially shines as much as the gloss, making it almost impossible to avoid misses, which would show as glossy spots. Touching up is always unsatisfactory, and if the eggshell varnish is retouched once it has settled down a flash will result, giving an unpleasant sheen. Best results are obtained with careful hair stippling.

Various grades of flat varnish are made from dead flat, matt and eggshell, to semi-gloss. The eggshell finish most nearly approximates to wax polish and with age and constant wiping with a cloth duster becomes almost indistinguishable.

For economical work flat varnishes are obtainable which require no preliminary gloss varnish, but they usually lack the depth and durability of the twofold process. Nearly all flat varnishes contain wax and should be thoroughly rubbed down to ensure adhesion when subsequently applying further coats.

High Quality Varnishing

In the past it was customary for coach painters to apply as many as six successive coats of varnish, flatting down between each coat, first with pumice powder, and then with successively finer powders such as putty powder (tin oxide), tripoli and crocus, and dry polishing the final coat with wheat flour. The author has within the last few years carried out this process over grey walnut graining in the boardroom of an important firm in one of the new towns. Expensive french polished bleached Italian walnut veneers used for the office furniture had to be matched.

Old Work

Re-varnishing old work may successfully be undertaken if it is in sound condition. Thorough preparation with sugar soap is essential, commencing from the base and working up to avoid discolouration from runs of the detergent, and rubbing down with fine glasspaper without scratching. Rinsing must be thorough to remove all traces of original dirt and detergent. When dry, touch up all defects with the appropriate stainers, which should be bound with a little of the finishing varnish and thinned with turps, softening into the surrounding work with the finger tip and rag. When dry the varnish coating can be applied in the same way as for new work.

Alternatively the touching up may be done after the varnish has partly set, but there is always the risk of runs leaving the blemish almost uncovered and a dark stain underneath. Special care must be taken where human grease has penetrated the work in the vicinity of door handles, on hand rails and newel posts, and it often pays to apply a thin coat of knotting beforehand to doubtful surfaces. Tacky varnish is an abomination and in extreme cases it may be desirable to add a little liquid dryers which should always be from the same maker as the varnish.

Old grained work that is light in colour may, after touching up, be glazed with an overgraining technique, using a well-thinned proprietary scumble. The one time popular light fumed oak may be modified to a rich Jacobean shade, preserving to some extent the original figuring. Trials should be made in unobtrusive places for approval. Even a thin wash has remarkable reviving powers, impossible to obtain without patchiness with a stained varnish. Varnish over the scumble may be either flat or glossy.

Light Varnishes

Special varnishes are made for light colours and wallpaper. For the latter extreme care is necessary, as varnish immediately blackens paper on contact. To avoid this, two coats of size must be applied, preferably in a cold, almost jellied condition, making sure that no misses occur. See that the pattern is undisturbed by the size. If this happens the paper is unsuitable for varnish. Plastic emulsion varnishes are of recent introduction and need no preliminary sizing. They have a moderate sheen and a fair degree of moisture resistance, but again trials for suitability should be made.

Various liquid wood finishes are available, providing excellent and varied protective films over plain or stained work and manufactured chipboards, etc., but are entirely unsuitable over painted grounds. Preservative wood stains are sometimes available in forms which may be varnished, but conventional decoration is impossible over creosote and many effective preservative solutions.

French Polish

French polish was the original furniture finish, and in skilled hands still provides the best of all wood finishes. It sometimes falls to the lot of the painter to carry out french polishing, always really a job for the specialist.

Briefly, the new work must be lightly glasspapered in the direction of the grain only, and if necessary filled, best perhaps in these days with a cellulose filler. Again rub down smooth and apply a coat of water or spirit stain to appropriate colour and intensity. Never use an oil stain. Water stain will raise the grain which will again have to be lightly papered. The safest way is to go over the surface beforehand with warm water to raise the grain, and glasspaper smooth when dry.

Next in a warm, dry atmosphere apply a coat of brush polish with a polisher's mop, a soft horse- or camel-hair round brush often mounted in quill. This must be spread quickly and evenly, as the polish, which is a solution of shellac in commercial alcohol or methylated spirit, dries rapidly. When dry, again glasspaper until perfectly smooth.

139

Next prepare a rubber from a pad of cotton-wool (Fig. 1), soaked in french polish to which a few drops of linseed oil have been added, enclosing the egg-shaped wadding with non-linting rag in such a way that gentle pressure squeezes a little polish through the rag. The rubber is worked over the surface with a progressive, systematic figure-of-eight movement, rubbing in as much as possible into the wood and never laying it on as with varnish. The rubber must remain on and glide over the work. Lifting creates a ridge, and when finishing or recharging is necessary, the pad should be gently slid from the surface. This process is known as bodying in. For the best work the rubber is used instead of the mop which is only employed for intricate detail and carving.

Fig. 1. POLISHING RUBBER USED IN
FRENCH POLISHING.

When the bodying in is dry, glasspaper again using No. o paper, and use half methylated spirit with the polish for the next application of the rubber, applied evenly and gently and try to work out the linseed oil which will cloud the gloss until finally eliminated. Final spiriting out is accomplished with the use of nearly all spirit mixed with a minimum of polish and requires great skill and care to avoid lifting the underlying film. Desist immediately the slightest pull is felt and allow ample drying time before attempting more spiriting out.

Repolishing Old Work

Old work in good condition may be thoroughly cleaned and re-polished, using spirit stain for touching up and suitably coloured beeswax for stopping (if required). If in poor condition, stripping must be undertaken, using a spirit remover or scraping with a joiner's steel scraper until all vestiges are removed. If a light finish or change of hue is required, bleaching may be necessary. This is usually accomplished by applying a concentrated solution of oxalic acid (spirits of lemon), obtaining the crystals (which are poisonous) from a chemist. Allow to dry for about 24 hours, in the sun if possible, and thoroughly rinse off.

Usually this is sufficient, but in obstinate cases a special bleach may be used. Two solutions are used; solution A is applied and when dry immediately followed by B. Again allow at least 24 hours and then thoroughly clean the surface by washing. Needless to say all remnants of polish must be eliminated before any bleach can affect the actual wood. When stripping and bleaching are satisfactorily accomplished, the polishing proceeds as for new work.

Many forms of polish are now on the market, and some, specially compounded for 'do it yourself', give excellent results provided that the directions are implicitly observed. Special heat- and spirit-resistant polishes, usually based on phenolic resins are available for table tops, bar counters, etc. Exterior polished work is sometimes protected with a coat of oil varnish, and for this the polish is finished in the usual way, but must be flatted with pumice powder to ensure adhesion of the varnish.

Wax Polish

Wax polishing is traditionally carried out by preparation as for french polishing. The polish itself is prepared by shredding pure bees wax, melting over hot water, and mixing into similarly warmed turpentine. When cool the resultant stiff but plastic wax is rubbed vigorously into the wood, a short, stiff scrubbing brush being excellent for this. The sheen is obtained by alternate polishing and rubbing in. A cloth enclosing the scrubbing brush is an excellent method of obtaining more pressure when polishing, completing with a velvet covered pad. Properly carried out with plenty of elbow grease an exceedingly beautiful and durable finish is obtained. All bleaching and staining should, of course, be carried out first. Ready made wax polishes require less labour but rarely equal the home-made product. For light woods bleached wax should be used. In large scale work electrical polishers replace the hard labour; large scale french polishing is undertaken by spraying.

13 Colour and Design

A KNOWLEDGE OF BASIC colour theory is invaluable to the decorator. There are many different theories, but in the limited space available only the simplest will be dealt with. Good colour sense, whether restrained or daring, is a measure of good taste reinforced with knowledge. A clear understanding of descriptive terms is essential, and, although the following definitions may appear somewhat arbitrary, they should be adhered to as far as possible. The word colour is often used indiscriminately and may mean anything from the actual hue to the paint itself. In the following text it will be used when necessary to conform with current practice.

HUE   *Quality of Colour*, e.g. Redness, yellowness, etc.
TINT   *Hue plus White.*
SHADE   *Hue plus Black.* (Pastel shades, Hue + black + white.)
TONE   *Depth.* (In terms of light and dark.)
SATURATION   *Degree of Intensity.*

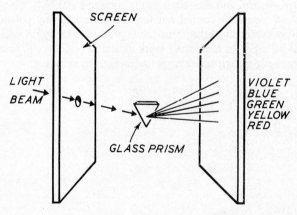

Fig. 1. HOW PRISM SPLITS UP WHITE LIGHT.

The Spectrum

The source of all colour is light itself. White light is composed of the complete range of visible hues with the addition of the invisible infra-red and ultra-violet rays, the latter being responsible for sun burn. When a beam of white light is directed through a glass prism, the component rays are refracted and

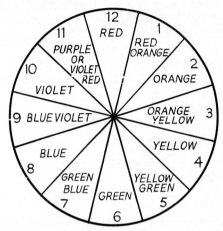

Fig. 2. THE COLOUR CIRCLE. Primary colours are red, yellow, and blue, and secondary colours orange, green, and violet.

split up and if projected on a screen appear as a coloured band known as the spectrum (Fig. 1). The short violet rays are deflected most, followed by blue, green, yellow, orange, and red, the longest visible. Everyone has seen nature's spectrum, the rainbow, in which the sun's rays are refracted by the raindrops acting as prismatic lenses. The predominant rainbow hues are reddish orange, through green to violet blue.

For convenience the hues of the spectrum may be represented as occupying segments of a circle, the simplest being divided into twelve as in the diagram Fig. 2, which shows the hues gradually merging from one to the other, and differing from the spectral band in that the violet returns through purple to red. The colour circle should be considered as a diagrammatic aid to theory rather than as a representation of scientific fact. It can be proved by experiment that, although most hues may be obtained by mixture, it is impossible to obtain red, yellow, or blue by any combination of hues. Because of this these three are known as *Primary Colours*. *Secondary Colours* are obtained by mixing two primaries; *Tertiary Colours* by mixing two secondaries as in Fig. 3.

Further additions will provide indifferent, muddy hues.

Hues which appear diametrically opposite in the colour circle are known

143

as *Complementary Colours*, and are opposite in all respects. For example, blue and orange have nothing in common; neither have green and red; or yellow and violet. Their complete contrast may be used with striking effect, as their juxtaposition enhances the hue of each. Red appears much more intense against green than its near neighbours in the colour circle, orange and purple. Complementary colours suggest each other and red placed against white tends to induce a greenish hue in the white; green would suggest a faint pink.

An interesting experiment is to stare at a brilliant red disc until the eye is thoroughly tired, cover it with white paper and a faint green disc will appear on the paper. This is due to the fact that the white light reflected by the paper contains all the spectral hues, but as the retina of the eye has become fatigued

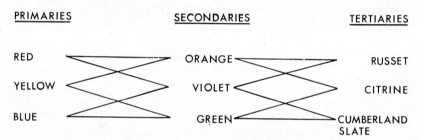

PRIMARIES	SECONDARIES	TERTIARIES

Fig. 3. HOW SECONDARY COLOURS ARE PRODUCED FROM PRIMARIES, AND TERTIARIES FROM SECONDARIES.

it fails to perceive the red rays, only the blue and yellow which produce the effect of green. Other complementaries act in the same way.

Split Complementaries are hues just each side of the true complementary, for example: blue violet and violet red may be considered as split complementaries to yellow. Hues adjacent to each other in the circle are known as *Analogous*, i.e. red and orange red, or even red and orange.

From the spectrum it will be seen that white is a combination of all the individual hues, as may be demonstrated by focusing a balanced mixture of red, blue, and yellow light on to a screen. If a circular card is coloured accurately progressing from red, through orange, yellow, green, blue, and violet, back to red as in the colour circle, and rapidly revolved round a centre pin, a nearly white card will appear. If the pigments were as pure as light rays and the correct sequence and intensity of hue were possible, the disc would become pure white, the eye accomplishing the actual blending. Black should be considered as a complete absence of colour. Actually pure black objects are only visible by means of their reflected light. Coloured surfaces owe their hue to their quality of absorbing all the rays except those of their intrinsic hue, which they reflect. A pure red ball reflects the red rays only, absorbing all the yellow and blue. A green ball reflects the blue and yellow rays only.

Another Theory

Some colour theorists such as *Munsell* have devised a colour circle based on ten instead of twelve divisions, resulting in slightly different complementaries, blue-green becoming the complementary of red and so on. Visually, in terms of light action on the retina, this may be nearer the truth. Mixtures of coloured light behave entirely differently from pigments, blue and orange light making white; blue and orange pigments, a brownish green. Impressionist artists utilized this phenomena by painting with little dabs of prismatic contrasting hues so closely placed that the eye did the blending instead of the artist on his palette. Brilliant sunlit effects were produced by this method of applying scintillating broken colour, and with modern artists the underlying principle is still observed, but with modification of the somewhat laboured dabbing, known as pointillism.

The colour circle cannot include greys and browns, and elaborate devices have been devised to include these and shades and tints. From such sources the system of British Standard Colour Charts have evolved. These define by numbers each hue, tint, and shade in the range. The colour charts of most manufacturers include many of these, sometimes all, in addition to their own subtle and delightful colours.

It has been said that there is no such thing as bad colour, only bad colour combinations. It will be noticed that the yellow end of the spectrum is naturally light in tone, darkening progressively towards the violet and one form of bad colour juxtaposition may be the contrast of a cool brown (really a yellow of low intensity) with a very pale blue or lavender, thus producing a discordant reversal of the natural tones of light yellow and deep blue or violet.

Harmonies are produced by the use of analogous colours, with accents provided by restrained use of complementaries. When using the colour circle as a basis for colour schemes, the nearest equivalent to the actual tints or shades to be used should be selected, i.e. yellow for creamy shades, violet for lavender, and so on. In this way it will be seen that pastel cream and lavender shades are complementary, but also harmonized by the presence of white and perhaps black in each. Pastel shades and greys readily harmonize, especially when of similar tone values as do also tones and shades of the same hue. Analogous colours harmonize but tend to weaken each other.

Many pastel shades may well be described as gleam colours; pale yellows, pinks, pale greens, blues, and lavenders are suggestive of delicate spring sunshine.

Good Colour Schemes

Successful colour schemes depend on many factors. First perhaps should come suitability for purpose considered with environment. Redecorations to a room must harmonize with existing furnishings, and, even if these are being renewed, the scheme must be designed as a whole. Aspect is also important; a sunny room may well be painted in cool blues and greens, whereas a north facing room will be more cheerful with warm buffs and browns. Lighting also plays its part, modern fluorescent tubes having a decided cooling effect on many hues. With warm colours predominating, ceilings should be warm tints of off white, cream, and so on to harmonize, using only dead or blued whites in conjunction with generally cool schemes. Beware of deep hues on ceilings as they normally receive somewhat less light than the remainder of the room and the large unbroken mass always accentuates the colour.

Modern Schemes

Contemporary decoration is a law unto itself; daring and sometimes even outrageous contrasts often come off with surprising success. Strong primrose ceilings, deep lilac walls, with white woodwork as a foil, combined with gay modern furnishings can provide exciting and stimulating surroundings. Such schemes are well adapted to the decoration of ultra-modern flats and houses, places of entertainment, and some types of shops. With the latter, care must be taken that the décor does not overwhelm the display of merchandise.

Proportion and form must be considered as an integral part of a colour scheme, and the relative sizes and shapes of the areas of contrasting colour must be taken equally into account. Many canons of proportion have been evolved, generally attempting to establish an over-all symmetry with the use of assymetrical parts. A square shape is generally considered to be less interesting than a rectangle, which again looks best when the length of adjacent sides are not in definite numerical relationship such as twice as long as wide. The theory of the golden mean postulates an ideal proportion as one is to the square root of two, the proportion of the side to the diagonal of a square. This approximates to 5 : to nearly 8, and a useful rough and ready progression of this subtle proportion may be expressed as—5 : 8 : 13 : 21 : 34, and so on, subtle and almost constant through the whole series. With a wall thirteen feet high, the dado at 5 feet would provide a much more attractive division than say 4 ft. 4 in. dado with 8 ft. 8 in. filling, too obviously two to one. This and similar subtle scales of proportion may be used to advantage in designing masses for painting or papering in different effects.

Two-paper Scheme

Contemporary paperhanging often includes the use of two or more contrasting papers in one room. A plain paper may cover all the walls leaving the chimney breast to be emphasized with a prominent pattern. Alternatively, opposite walls may be hung with one paper and the other two with another. There is always the danger, when one paper is obviously much more expensive than the other, of creating the impression that the owner could not afford to use the dearer paper for the whole room. A not-so-young prospective tenant of a new L.C.C. flat did actually remark 'It's a pity that the L.C.C. could not afford the same paper all the way round.'

Sometimes attractive effects are obtained by hanging patterned papers in the corners of a room, with the remainder in geometrically figured or plain papers. This often solves a problem when dealing with out-of-plumb angles, an over-all pattern masking irregularities that could not be concealed by a striped or squared paper. Charming effects used to be obtained by panelling with stiling borders, sometimes enhanced with cut-out corner decorations. Applied wallpaper decorations in the form of landscape, flower groupings, etc., were once popular and may return with changing fashions.

As with paint, colour of wallpaper is most important. Large patterns and aggressive colours tend to reduce the size of a room, horizontals increase the length, decreasing the height, and vertical stripes markedly increase the apparent height. A deep frieze lowers an over-high ceiling and sometimes rescues a small room from a box shaped appearance. As a rule warm colours advance, and cool blues (by suggesting distance) recede and add a feeling of spaciousness.

In the best taste, decorations should be planned to harmonize with the period of the house. By all means indulge in contemporary schemes in modern open-plan houses and flats, thus providing a background for cocktails, snacks, and brittle wit, in contrast with the Victorian drawing-room with its aura of port and serious conversation. A music room designed for the performance of traditional chamber music should be designed entirely differently to one intended for modern dissonances of jazz. If an endeavour is made to exercise one's own taste within these limits little can go wrong. Never try 'To keep up with the Joneses', or, worse still, to go one better. Because a neighbour has painted the outside of his house in aggressive red, there is no justification in making matters worse by retaliating with an offensive blue.

Exterior Schemes

External painting colours may be gay and attractive without vulgarity. Always remember that the household and guests alone have to endure interior decorations, but the contemplation of exterior decorations is shared by every passer-by. Generally speaking, exterior painting should be related to the period of the house, especially with windows and gutters. On a Georgian, Victorian, or Edwardian house, the traditional white for the sashes, stone colour for the frames and perhaps green for the gutters and pipes, is still eminently suitable, with gay gleam colours for the doors. To be really traditional, grain the doors in oak. It is a pity that the respective owners of semi-detached houses do not more often agree on a mutual treatment. Nothing looks worse than one half of a gable painted one colour and the other half another, divided by a none too straight line at the top mitre.

Period Work

Period houses warrant period decoration. Early English with its gothic forms, Tudor and Jacobean with tapestried and panelled walls and renaissance plastered ornament, Queen Anne with its classical forms enhanced by Chinese design which continued to distinguish Georgian from its Palladian origin. Victorian design, which is due for a revival, was at its best solid and comfortable, but, at its worst often over ornate and pretentious.

At the beginning of this century a florid, sinuous design encompassed everything. This romantic short-lived style was designated 'L'arte Noveau' and was probably conceived as a derivative from the pre-Raphaelites and such fine designers as William Morris, without any real appreciation of their artistic aims. If period decorations have to be undertaken, study from such great examples of the Tudor as Hampton Court, the Palladian of Blenheim Palace, and the other great examples of English architecture.

If an elaborate scheme is being undertaken, preliminary water colour perspectives may avoid a great deal of frustration. It is much easier to make a few different drawings than to repaint a whole mansion. Many of the larger paint and paper manufacturers employ designing artists who prepare the simplest and most elaborate schemes in answer to bona-fide requests.

14 Faults and Remedies. Special Equipment

IF ALL DECORATIVE work were carried out under ideal conditions with good and appropriate materials and competent workmanship, little could go wrong until age and exposure had taken its toll. Unfortunately these conditions seldom completely obtain, and in any case even the skilled decorator may not be aware of the trouble likely to occur when working over originally badly prepared and finished work. Unfortunately, by the solvent action of thinners and mediums, old, apparently sound coatings may be chemically and physically reactivated by freshly applied coatings, breaking down original adhesion, or setting up a train of destructive physico-chemical reactions as disastrous as the chain reaction of an atomic explosion. As suggested earlier in this book, if in any doubt, remove old paint entirely and start again. In the long run this will prove far more economical than any attempts to 'put right'.

PAINTED SURFACES

Fault	Cause	Cure
Blistering.	Presence of moisture, vapour, or, unoxydized oils and resins.	Burn off or chemically remove.
Flaking. Cracking.	As above, and failure to break down old surface and secure adhesion. Underbound undercoats. Gloss on gloss.	Remove as necessary.
Curtaining. Creeping. Wrinklings.	Too liberal and/or uneven application	Rub down to sound base.

Fault	*Cause*	*Cure*
Blooming.	Condensation in the form of water, fog or frost, during drying period.	Avoid application in damp or cold, otherwise rub down and re-coat.
Crocodile Leather Effect.	Hard inelastic paint over soft elastic or partly dried paint.	Rub down to sound base if inactive, otherwise remove.
Bleeding.	Oil soluble dye pigments, tar and bitumen present.	Remove as much as possible, treat with two coats styptic knotting.
Saponification.	Presence of alkali plaster not dried out.	Wash off, allow time for neutralization. Prime with alkali-resist.
Tackiness. Slow or Non-Drying.	Presence of grease, oil, or alkali.	Remove. May sometimes be coated with a special drying medium, a doubtful cure.
Grittiness.	Dust, dirty paint containers and brushes. Excess dryers.	Rub down and re-coat.

DISTEMPERED SURFACES

Fault	*Cause*	*Cure*
Flaking.	Failure to remove old loosely adhering distemper. Incompatible coatings. Too many coats.	Remove by scrubbing and scraping. Prime with sealer and fill. Lining paper.
Staining.	Moisture penetration. Rain. Grease and chemicals. Stale size.	Remove and seal. Lining paper.

Fault	Cause	Cure
Efflorescence. (Powdery incrustation).	Crystallization of salts working out from background, bricks, etc.	Brush off, leave and brush off again until no more appears. Do not wash, as moisture will dissolve crystals and force them into background.
Flashing.	Careless application. 'Hot' Plaster.	Wash off and prepare with Clearcolle for soft distemper. Add petrifying liquid to washable.
Cracks Opening.	Failure to cut out, and/or wet in. Poor stopping.	Cut out, wet in and stop, touch up and re-coat.

PAPERED SURFACES

Fault	Cause	Cure
Blisters.	Insufficient soaking. Poor hanging.	May be possible to damp and roll out.
Lifted Edges.	Poor pasting and hanging.	Lift, re-paste, leave to soften, then re-fix.
Shrinkage at Joints.	Hung over painted or impervious surface without rubbing down.	None. May be avoided by well rubbing down, sizing and cross lining.
Stains.	Careless pasting and hanging.	Possibly damping and applying blotting-paper.
Damp.	Moisture penetration. Condensation.	Remove cause. Re-paper.

151

The foregoing lists of faults should be useful for quick reference, but in some cases the brief tabulations are hardly adequate. In cases of blistering and flaking, moisture may penetrate from behind, and often occurs on the rails of sashes to kitchens and bathrooms (Fig. 1), and also on the middle rail of garage

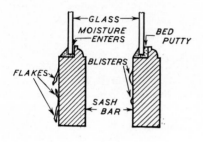

Fig. 1. HOW MOISTURE CAUSES FLAKING AND BLISTERING.

doors, which are for some unknown reason glazed inside out. Condensation or rainwater in the latter case, runs down the glass, penetrating the bed putty, soaks into the wood, and eventually finds its way out the front, often tremendously expanded to vapour by the heat of the sun. Again the cure lies in removing the cause by re-bedding the glass in a watertight manner.

The focussing of the sun's rays through windows or the proximity of fires and boilers may volatilize the natural water content of the wood. When this has happened, removal and repainting usually effects a cure. Pipes containing hot water should always be treated with heat-resisting paint. Resinous woods are prone to blistering and flaking, and should always be primed with aluminium primer. Obstinate cases have sometimes been cured by priming the bare wood with washable distemper before applying a normal coat of priming. This seems to act as a buffer coat, not being elastic enough to stretch into a blister, but with a tendency to flake instead.

Faults in Materials

Paint faults often arise from failure to stir properly, thus failing to secure a homogeneous mix of medium, dryers, pigment, and thinners. The heavier constituents often sink to the bottom of the container, and some of these may have a most important part to play in the eventual life of the paint. In extreme cases it may be necessary to add dryers, but these should always be from the same maker as the paint and used as sparingly as possible. Their effect is continuous and in time, all elasticity is destroyed.

Trouble can sometimes occur through using pigments which react chemically with each other. Stainers containing sulphur should never be mixed with lead paints which are blackened by the formation of lead sulphide.

This may sometimes be remedied by the application of peroxide of hydrogen, which changes the black sulphide to the white sulphate. White lead may also 'chalk' prematurely. The addition of just a little ochre for some reason seems to check this.

Blooming

Blooming is troublesome in autumn and winter, and no finishing work should be undertaken after mid-day when mist or frost seems likely at night. With gloss paints it is a fairly simple matter (though expensive), to rub down and re-coat, but sometimes much more difficult to rectify overgrained and varnished work. The bloom resembles minute crystals of camphor which break up and reflect light in all directions, destroying gloss and presenting an opaque milky surface. Sometimes it is possible to restore transparency by re-varnishing, but, failing this, buffing out and re-graining will be necessary.

Crocodile leather effects are artificially produced by spraying rapid hard drying cellulose finishes over elastic, slow drying undercoats, producing the

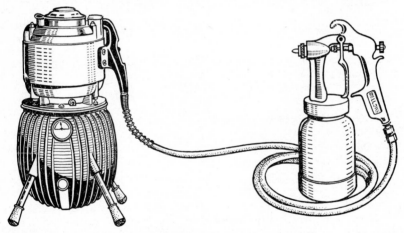

Fig. 2. EQUIPMENT FOR SPRAYING.

well-known industrial crackle finishes. Spraying and the use of industrial finishes are somewhat outside the scope of the ordinary decorator and must be the subject of another volume, but, quite briefly, reasonably good jobs can be carried out with moderately priced equipment ranging from about £50 upwards. Masking is most important, and the suppliers' directions should be implicitly followed. Adhesive masking tape should be used when working to definite boundaries, covering the remainder with Polythene sheets. Fig. 2 shows spraying apparatus.

Roller Application

Application by roller is quick and efficient for painting large surfaces of all kinds, but cannot be used right into angles without the use of an angle roller or brush, the latter often giving a marked difference in texture. The rollers

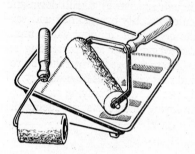

Fig. 3. ROLLERS AND CHARGING TRAY.

may be coated with lambs' wool or plastic foam, and must be thoroughly cleaned after use with one of the modern brush cleansers. For small jobs the brush is probably as quick when the time occupied in cleaning, etc., is taken into account. Figs. 3–5 show apparatus and its use.

Special Apparatus

Steam strippers are useful for removing heavy coatings of wallpaper and old distemper. Steam is generated and conveyed by tube to a handled plate which held close to the wall ejects steam at high pressure. Many layers may be removed with the stripping knife at one operation once penetration is complete.

A small but useful adjunct is tack rag. This usually in the form of an impregnated pad which lifts dust from work and retains it, thus preventing dust from flying about and settling on other finished work. It can be used for some time before renewal becomes necessary.

Special agitating machines are available for re-mixing old paint which has settled badly, but if new purchases are in such condition they should be returned to the makers. Certain emulsions and glossy distempers deteriorate rather rapidly and there is often a time limit printed on the container stipulating the latest date on which the material may be used. Paint mills for power or hand grinding are almost a thing of the past, but may prove useful for regrinding old paints together to form a rough ironwork paint known as

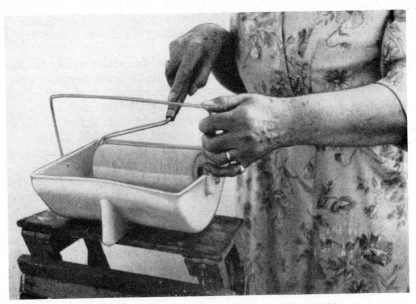

Fig. 4. CHARGING PAINT ROLLER IN TRAY.

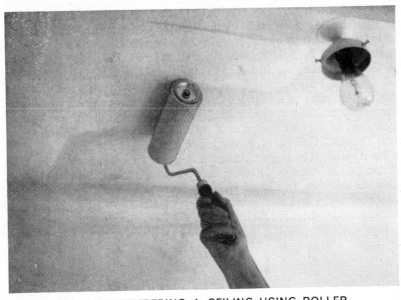

Fig. 5. DISTEMPERING A CEILING USING ROLLER.

smudge. Years ago this use of old paint was common practice, but with so many formulae used in manufacture, the mixing of different brands may be dangerous, resulting in a useless product.

Patent graining rollers and combs are available which rapidly produce oak effects with varying degrees of success. In skilled hands they may be used for cheap work, but the figure is always repetitive and lacks the variety and interest of good hand work. Absorbent raised grain patterns may be cut to size and rolled on to the wet graining colour and when removed leave an imprint of the figure, which can after be softened and modified. This process, although accurately reproducing the characteristics of various fine timbers, is lacking in the essential charm of hand work.

Wallpaper trimming machines may be hand or electrically operated, trimming both edges and re-winding automatically. When large amounts of paperhanging are undertaken they can prove very economical, but seldom deal with relief papers with complete satisfaction. The skilled craftsman still prefers a good hand trimmer or the knife and straight-edge. Special paste boards are available with a paste container underneath which automatically unroll, paste trim and cut at one operation, but have never become specially popular.

Much useful equipment may be improvised, such as placing two sets of pasteboards side by side when dealing with wide materials such as the modern poly-vinyl cloths hung as wall decorations. When hanging these mural fabrics, the walls or other surfaces must be prepared to a suction-free finish, and the special adhesive applied to them and the dry material rolled on. True butts are obtained by overlapping, laying a straight-edge down the lap, and cutting through both thicknesses with a sharp knife, tearing off the excess.

Good decorating is achieved by the exercise of first-class skill coupled with full technical knowledge and artistic feeling. In the past these have been obtained by years of hard work and experience, often gained by trial and error. The budding craftsman can, today, profit by all the accumulated knowledge of the past and present, by undertaking a course of study at his local Technical College, where every facility, practical and theoretical will be at his disposal. Thorough technical ability and knowledge will bring satisfaction and pleasure in designing and executing the humblest to the most elaborate schemes. In the old days the terms *painter* and *artist* were used indiscriminately, and the craftsman's aim should be to justify the original meaning of the fine word PAINTER.

WALLPAPER TABLE

For Finding the Number of Pieces of Wallpaper, English size, required for any Room

Measure round the Four Walls in feet, including Doors, Windows, etc.

Length of Four Walls in Feet

Height in feet from Skirting to Cornice or Picture Rail	28	32	36	40	44	48	52	56	60	64	68	72	76	80	84	88	92	96	100 round room
7 and under 7½	4	4	4	4	6	6	7	7	8	8	8	9	9	10	10	11	11	12	12
7½ ,,	4	4	5	5	6	6	7	8	8	9	9	10	10	11	12	12	12	13	13
8 ,,	4	5	5	5	6	7	7	8	8	9	9	10	10	11	12	12	13	13	14
8½ ,,	4	5	5	6	7	7	8	8	9	9	10	11	11	12	12	13	13	14	14
9 ,,	4	5	6	6	7	7	8	9	9	10	10	11	12	12	13	13	14	15	15
9½ ,,	5	5	6	7	7	8	9	9	10	11	11	12	12	13	14	14	15	15	16
10 ,,	5	6	6	7	8	8	9	10	10	11	12	12	13	14	14	15	16	16	17
10½ ,,	5	6	7	7	8	9	9	10	11	11	12	13	13	14	15	16	16	17	18
11 ,,	5	6	7	8	8	9	10	10	11	11	13	14	13	15	16	16	17	18	18
11½ ,,	5	7	7	8	9	10	10	11	12	12	13	14	14	15	16	17	17	18	18

(100 round room column = pieces of paper)

CEILING PAPERS

TABLE TO MEASURE CEILINGS FOR PAPER

For use in Average Rooms, but not for Passages, etc.

Measurement in Feet Round Four Walls of Room	20 to 28	30 to 40	42 to 48	52 to 58	60 to 66	68 to 70	72 to 78	80 to 82	84 to 88	90 to 92	94 to 98	100 to 104
No. of Pieces required	1	2	3	4	5	6	7	8	9	10	11	12

Index